THE PATHWAY TO ASCENSION

VOLUME ONE

Thank you for supporting independent publishing and the Systemology Society.

mardukite.com

MARDUKITE ACADEMY OF SYSTEMOLOGY COLLECTOR'S EDITION

THE PATHWAY TO ASCENSION

SPIRITUAL CLEARING VOLUME ONE

*Systemology Professional Course
presented by Joshua Free*

© 2023, JOSHUA FREE

ISBN : 978-1-961509-33-7

All Rights Reserved. No part of this publication may be reproduced in any form or by any means, electronic or mechanical, including photocopying, recording, artificial intelligence databases or systems, without permission from the publisher. This book is a religious artifact. It is not intended to diagnose any illness or substitute any medical treatment or professional health advice.

A MARDUKITE SYSTEMOLOGY PUBLICATION

Mardukite Research Library Catalogue No. "Liber-5A"

Developed for Mardukite Academy & The Systemology Society

cum superiorum privilegio veniaque

FIRST EDITION
December 2023

Published from
Joshua Free Imprint – JFI Publications
Mardukite Borsippa HQ, San Luis Valley, Colorado

Chart Your Flight For Ascension...
Then Let Your Spirit Fly!

Unlock your ultimate spiritual potential by removing the barriers to your true native state. Learn how to easily attain *Self-Actualization* and even help actualize others along the way. A greater appreciation and understanding of *Spiritual Life* and *Existence* awaits you. Expand your reach to achieve your dreams.

Each 'Professional Course' lesson offers simple exercises and techniques that directly apply the metahuman philosophy of Systemology, assisting to increase your true *Knowingness*, improve your capabilities in this life, and even decide what you will do in your next.

This collector's edition hardcover includes the first eight (of sixteen) lesson-booklets for the "*Pathway to Ascension*" Professional Course, including *Systemology Processing Levels 0 to 3*. At the Mardukite Academy of Systemology, the 'Professional Course' lessons in this series are presented to Seeker's that have already completed the 'Basic Course', previously released as six lesson-booklets, or the six-in-one single volume edition "*Fundamentals of Systemology.*"

This professional presentation of the official Systemology 'Pathway-to-Ascension' takes new Seekers and continuing students from "*Zero*" to "*Infinity*" at lightning-fast speeds!

Discover Who You Really Are...
Because You Were Never Human!

The first eight (of sixteen) lessons from the Complete 2023 Professional Course for The Systemology Pathway-to-Ascension in one Collector's Edition Hardcover.

MARDUKITE SYSTEMOLOGY SOCIETY
"THE PATHWAY TO ASCENSION"
PROFESSIONAL COURSE
VOLUME ONE

- Introduction to the Professional Course ... 13
- A New View of the Human Spirit ... 14
- Studying the Professional Course ... 16
- Charting a Course on the Pathway ... 18
- Taking Flight on the Pathway ... 20

.... ONE ....
:: INCREASING AWARENESS ::
- First Flights on the Pathway ... 25
- Self-Directing Attention ... 25
- Advanced Applications ... 29
- Helpful Tips on Processing ... 31
- "Touch-and-Let-Go" ... 35
- Willingness to Reach ... 37
- "The Wall" ... 39
- The Beta-Awareness Scale ... 40
- The Formal Session Example Script ... 41

.... TWO ....
:: THOUGHT & EMOTION ::
- Keeping a Flight Log ... 49
- Control of Mind and Body ... 50
- Associative Identification ... 51
- Creating Emotional Flows ... 53
- Automation and Reactivity ... 55
- Confronting "As-It-Is" ... 58
- Introducing Subjective Processing ... 61
- Basic Subjective Processing ... 64
- Confronting the Past ... 66
- Analytical Recall ... 68

THREE
:: CLEAR COMMUNICATION ::
– Willingness to Reach Further . . . 73
– Expanding Willingness . . . 75
– Systemology and Communication . . . 78
– Communication Processes . . . 81
– Acknowledgment Processes . . . 84
– Duplication and Reproduction . . . 85
– "Bell, Book and Candle" . . . 87

FOUR
:: HANDLING HUMANITY ::
– Handling the Human Condition . . . 93
– Communication and Protest . . . 94
– "Protest" Defragmentation . . . 96
– Acceptance and Rejection . . . 99
– Change and Motion . . . 101
– Processing "Change" . . . 103
– Human Problems . . . 106
– Defragmenting "Problems" . . . 109
– On the Subject of "Help" . . . 112
– "Help" Defragmentation . . . 113

FIVE
:: FREE YOUR SPIRIT ::
– Releasing the Spirit . . . 119
– Spiritual Beingness . . . 120
– "Zu-Vision" and Processing . . . 122
– Locational "POV" Processing . . . 124
– Advanced Applications . . . 127
– "Creation-of-Space" . . . 128
– The "Musts" and "Can'ts" of Life . . . 131
– Defragmentation Techniques . . . 133
– "Avoiding" and "Getting Rid Of" . . . 138

SIX
:: ESCAPING SPIRIT-TRAPS ::
– Being at Cause . . . 143
– Basic Processing . . . 144

- Processing "Invalidation" . . . 148
- "Hostile-Acts" and "Hold-Outs" . . . 151
- "Spirit-Traps" and "Reality" . . . 154
- Some Basic Techniques . . . 157
- Escaping the Traps . . . 160
- Reaching Further . . . 163

. . . . SEVEN . . . .
:: ELIMINATING BARRIERS ::

- "Games" and "Barriers" . . . 167
- Fragmentation and "Barriers" . . . 168
- Processing "Barriers" . . . 171
- Defragmenting the "Flow-Factors" . . . 175
- Handling the "Flow-Factors" . . . 180
- More on "Barriers" . . . 185
- Advanced Processing . . . 188

. . . . EIGHT . . . .
:: CONQUEST OF ILLUSION ::

- Personal Integrity . . . 193
- "Confusion" and "Falsehood" . . . 194
- Defragmenting "Falsehood" . . . 196
- Handling "Suppression" . . . 200
- Defragmenting "Suppression" . . . 202
- "Justification" and "Responsibility" . . . 207
- Defragmenting "Justification" . . . 209

. . . . APPENDIX . . . .

- Systemology Glossary . . . 216
- Suggested Reading . . . 238

This material is continued in:
The Pathway to Ascension (Volume Two)

Systemology "Basic Level" Core Books
Fundamentals of Systemology (Basic Course)
The Power of Zu
Systemology: The Original Thesis

Systemology "Master Level" Core Books
The Tablets of Destiny Revelation
Crystal Clear: Handbook for Seekers
Metahuman Destinations (2 Volumes)

Systemology "Wizard Level" Core Books
Imaginomicon
The Way of the Wizard
Systemology-180: A Fast-Track to Ascension
Systemology: Backtrack

∞

EDITOR'S NOTE

"The Self does not actualize Awareness
past a point not understood."
—*Tablets of Destiny*

This book contains a collection of materials from
eight of the lesson-booklets developed by Joshua Free
for the "Pathway to Ascension" Professional Course.

A clear understanding of this material is critical for
achieving actual realizations and personal benefit
from applying our philosophy as spiritual technology.

Any time you run across an unfamiliar term,
refer to the "Systemology Glossary" in the appendix.
It is also helpful to keep a quality dictionary nearby.

The *Seeker* should not to simply "read through" this
book without practicing the "exercises" given and
attaining proper comprehension as "knowledge."
Even when the information continues to be
"interesting"—if at any point you find yourself feeling
lost or confused while reading, trace your steps back.
Return to the point of misunderstanding and go
through it again.

Take nothing within this book on faith.
Apply the information directly to your life.

Decide for yourself.

∞

WELCOME, SEEKER!
LET'S CHART YOUR JOURNEY ON THE PATHWAY

Systemology is a "holistic" approach to understanding the human experience. It is not actually a singular "subject" in itself, but rather, a new way in which to view the many subjects of *Life* and all *Existence*.

This is a professional course in *Systemology*—specifically, how to *apply* the spiritual philosophy of *Mardukite Systemology* as a personal *"Pathway" to Ascension*. Our *Systemology* is a new approach to *"Self-Actualization."* It is completely relevant for the modern age and the future; and quite different from any previous similar attempts, or other traditions, you might find. What's more: it is applicable to anyone with any background.

This *"Professional Course"* series of lessons immediately follows the material given in the *"Basic Course"* series—available as six separate pocket-sized booklets, or in a single hardcover volume titled: *"Fundamentals of Systemology: A New Thought For The 21st Century."*

This is a *new* presentation of *Systemology*, emphasizing the application of our philosophy for those *Seekers* that are *"Flying-Solo"*—or else working through their studies and exercises as solitary practitioners. This is a new innovation for *Systemology*. Aside from the book *"Crystal Clear,"* all of our former advanced courses have placed a focus on *"Traditional Piloting"*—where experienced practitioners assist *Seekers* in *"processing."*

To receive the greatest benefit from this study: it is expected that a *Seeker* will already be familiar with the fundamental concepts and terminology (previously relayed in the *Basic Course*) before using lessons from the *Professional Course*. This will allow us to cover the extensive territory of the *Pathway* much more quickly. However, for reference, a basic "*glossary*" of vocabulary used in this lesson is provided in the "*appendix*."

A NEW VIEW OF THE HUMAN SPIRIT

Systemology is not a religion and does not require any type of *faith*. It is, however, built upon a "spiritual" premise—and as such is an "applied spiritual philosophy." It is based on ancient teachings that we are *Spiritual Beings* essentially "wearing" bodies like clothes—or using them as "vehicles." Yet our true native nature is not *physical*, but beyond this existence; and we can certainly operate a "body" from *outside* of it.

We are **all** *Spiritual Beings*—each of us a *unit* of *Spiritual Awareness*—that have experienced a very long *Spiritual Timeline* of existence. Although we might be particularly attached to the familiar "physical shells" associated with *this* lifetime, our true "*Spiritual Lifetime*" is seemingly *eternal*. We have been many things before *Human*, and we go onward as a *Spiritual Being* after our "*genetic vehicle*" of *this* incarnation perishes.

While a "spiritual" view of the *Human Condition* may not seem unique to our philosophy, just how often is the concept treated *systematically*? For that matter: just how many people, supposedly raised to this or that religion, or professing to believe one thing or another, actually live their lives as though they are *Spirits*?

As *Spiritual Beings* of immortal existence and infinite potential, we are not simply the *"creations"* of an even greater *Beingness*; we are, in fact, an integral part of that *"creative force"* which permeates all existence.

Our basic nature is to be a *"creative being"*—our highest goals are *"to create."* And as such a being—which we refer to as an *Alpha-Spirit* in *Systemology*—we have run into some difficulties along the course of our *Spiritual Timeline* and found ourselves trapped within material *Universes* of our own collaborative *creation*.

Since we did not start out our existence in a trapped condition, it is correct to say that we have *"fallen"* from our native *"godlike"* states. It did not happen all at one, but progressively and systematically. We know our "troubles" have resulted from accumulated "barriers" and "blockages"—or *fragmentation*—during our vast experiences as *Spiritual Beings*. They are not because we lack something; but because of what's been added.

In *Systemology*, we systematically examine those routes by which we must have descended to reach our present condition, then reverse the direction of travel and chart a personal *"Pathway to Ascension."* Of course, the exact "details" of the *Spiritual Timeline* will be different for each individual *Seeker*. However, we have been able to systematically chart our *Pathway* based on common patterns of *Human fragmentation*.

In the most basic terms: the *fragmentation* that defines our "downward spiral" consists of decisions or considerations where we deny our true nature. This includes those decisions to *"withdraw"* rather than *"reach"*; where we choose to *not-know* rather than *know*; to *not-communicate* rather than *communicate*; and ultimately, to take *no-resp-*

onsibility for being a *creative-cause*, and therefore succumb to being an *effect*.

But there is *hope!* And much more importantly: there is an effectively workable *way out* of the mazes and traps of our existence. If you are reading this now, you have already begun to gather your tools and build up the *"horsepower"* necessary to break the gravity holding your *Spiritual Beingness* to the *Human Condition*.

STUDYING THE PROFESSIONAL COURSE

Most *Seekers* study and practice *Systemology* at-a-distance and independent of the "Mardukite Academy" or any "Master-level" mentors trained therein. This means that the *books* (and to a lesser degree, the *internet*) are the only means of direct contact a *Seeker* maintains with the "Systemology Society" during their studies. A continuing *Seeker* from the *"Basic Course"* will be familiar with the style of study found in *this* course.

Misunderstood words are the most common reason an individual abandons studying a subject. When a misunderstanding occurs, *Awareness* declines. These misunderstandings start to "stack up" after the first occurrence, and as a result, the level of interest and attention will also decline. This is how a "confusion" develops; and the individual will get "bored" with the subject, feel tired, and unable to concentrate.

One solution is to return to the part of the material that was still interesting and enjoyable to read. When scanning around that area of text, there is likely to be a new word (or new specific use of a familiar word) that is unclear, but was passed by unnoticed. All *Systemology* books include their own *glossary*. Using this *glossary* and a high-quality dictionary will help resolve this misunderstanding once it is located.

An effective education of any subject is taught on a *gradient*. This is what is intended by presenting the study of something as "*grades*." Rather than treating a subject as one total mass, true learning is achieved by increasing one's understanding with a *gradual* increase upward. The *ascent* to a mountaintop is not successfully achieved in one leap, but by targeting and reaching specific checkpoints along the way.

This *Professional Course* consists of a series of lessons that gradually increase a *Seeker's* ability to understand and apply the practices and techniques of *Systemology* as a complete "*Pathway to Ascension.*" It is an appropriate study for continuing *Seekers* (from the *Basic Course*), but also "advanced" *Systemologists*.

Each lesson of the *Professional Course* applies *Systemology* to a particular subject (or focus). It is best if the entire course can be studied and applied in sequential order. These lessons also employ a style of practice or technique called "*Systematic Processing.*" An introduction to applying this methodology is provided in the final lesson (booklet) of the *Basic Course*—or in the "*Fundamentals of Systemology*" volume.

To study the *Professional Course* just like a student at the Academy: a *Seeker* reads through all instructional material and applies each exercise (or "*process*") presented in the text to the extent they comfortably can, before continuing on to the next lesson.

When first starting on the *Pathway* as a *Solo* practitioner, without the aid of an experienced *Pilot*, a *Seeker* shouldn't "push too hard" or allow themselves to get too "stuck" on any one area (lesson) or *process*. It is not expected that any one area will be completely handled when first introduced. For optimum results, it is expected that a serious *Seeker* will make more than one "pass" through the entire *Professional Course*.

The *Professional Course* is not altogether different from other forms of practical or technical education: where the instruction and exercises are delivered to a completion, and then a student further increases their abilities, strength and skill-level by applying additional practice throughout their life. Therefore, a student should not concern themselves with perfectly mastering each step (or lesson) before progressing forward.

Additional passes through the material are likely to result in different *"realizations"* (an increased *level of understanding*) than a previous time. New "layers" of *Knowingness* may now be accessible during a *process* that may not have been before. It is important to avoid invalidating the progress you've made just because one area is not completely handled right away, or if a certain *process* seems too difficult on the first pass.

CHARTING A COURSE ON THE PATHWAY

Although we can communicate a systematic structure to *fragmentation,* the personal journey experienced along the *Pathway* will be different for each *Seeker*. For example, certain areas will seem more *"turbulent"* or difficult for one *Seeker* than another. We tend to say that these areas have more "*charge*" on them—or that they are more "*heavily charged.*" It is best to handle such areas when you are already feeling "good" and not in a situation (or condition) where that specific area is consistently being "*triggered*" or "*restimulated.*"

As an applied philosophy, *Systemology* "theory" can be easily utilized in the "laboratory" of the "world-at-large" in everyday life. This is implied within the basic instruction of each lesson. Unlike other "sciences" that conduct experiments by making a change to some "objective variable" *out there* and waiting to see an effect, our focus is the individual (or *Observer*) themselves, and how *they* affect the "*Reality*" perceived.

In addition to applying *Systemology* "New Thought" to everyday life, our philosophy is applied by using specific exercises and systematic techniques. These "*processes*" provide the most stable personal gain (and *realizations*) for each area; but only when actually applied with a *Seeker's* full "*presence*" and *Awareness*.

This *Professional Course* is designed so that it may be easily read and studied with little concern for what "dangers" these teachings—or *processing*—might unleash. However, there are still some guidelines that pertain to the "best-uses" of these course lessons, particularly if a *Seeker* intends for stable development.

Skipping over too much material/*processing* in early lessons may make attempts to understand (or apply) later lessons more difficult. However, once the complete *Professional Course* is worked through at least once in its entirety, specific areas can then be later returned to and treated with a greater sense of *Awareness* and "*presence*" than before. Of course, in "*Traditional Piloting,*" the rate of processing is monitored by an experienced practitioner; but in "*Solo-Processing,*" a *Seeker* must regulate their own progress on the *Pathway*.

Applying a systematic technique is called "*running a process.*" The *processes* are designed with very simple instructions or "*command-lines.*" To *run* a *processing command-line*, a *Seeker* may be assisted by the communication of that *line* from a "*Co-Pilot*" (as in "*Traditional Piloting*"). But even then, a *Seeker* must still personally "input" the *command* as *Self*. For this reason—and quite thankfully—*Solo-Processing* is possible.

TAKING FLIGHT ON THE PATHWAY

Processing Techniques are intended to treat the *Spiritual Being* or *Alpha-Spirit*; the individual themselves. It is applied by the *Alpha-Spirit*—then *Self-directed* to the "Mind-System" or even a "body" (*genetic-vehicle*), both of which are "constructs" that the *Alpha-Spirit* (*Self*, or the "I-AM" *Awareness unit*) operates, but neither of which is actually *Self*. *Fragmentation* causes *Humans* to falsely identify *Self as* the "*Mind*" or even a "*Body*."

The *Professional Course* lessons are designed for the *Beginning Seeker* in mind—one that may have an understanding of theory, but with little experience in practice. That being said: each of these lessons may be used toward total *Beta-Defragmentation* within a specific area. There are also more *processes* given for each subject than may be necessary to achieve an *ultimate end-point realization* on that entire area.

Some *processes* can be treated quite lightly at first; others may require a bit of working at in order to get *"running"* well. It is important to set aside a period of time when you can be dedicated to your studies and *processing*. This period of time is referred to as a *"processing session."* The reason for this, is that when a *process* does start *running* well, it is important to be able to complete it to a satisfactory *"end-point."*

The purpose of *systematic processing* is to be able to *really* "look" at things and even determine the *considerations* we have made—or attitudes we have decided—about *Reality* as a result of those experiences. It doesn't do us much good to simply "glance"—or to *restimulate* something uncomfortable and then quickly *withdraw* from it once again, leaving more of our *attention* yet again behind and held fixedly on it.

Generally speaking, a Seeker continues to *run* a *process* so long as something is "happening"—which is to say, the *process* is still producing a change. Usually this is evident by the type of "answers" that a *command-line* helps a Seeker originate from the database of their own *Mind-System*. The *command-lines* do not "do" anything on their own. They assist a Seeker to direct their own attention toward increasing *Awareness.*

Of course, a Seeker may also cease to generate new "data" from a *process* without reaching an *"ultimate" realization* as an *"end-point."* It is possible that additional "layers" (or even other "areas") require handling before anything "deeper" is accessible. If this is the case, end the *process*. But, if a Seeker is *withdrawing* from something uncomfortable that was incited or stirred up, then a *process* is *run* until they feel "good" about it.

In case the thought of encountering "*turbulence*" is a concern: the techniques given as "*Opening Procedures*" of a *Formal Session* (in the *Basic Course*), and those found in the earliest lessons of the *Professional Course*, are quite useful when applied as "safety nets" for maintaining *Awareness* and *presence*, even when *Flying-Solo*.

One of the benefits to *Flying-Solo* is that *processing* is entirely *Self-determined*. This already provides a certain built-in "safe-ty" for a practitioner. Anything you *restimulate* by *Self-determinism* is *your thing*. It is not incited by external *other-determined* influences (or other "source-points" in existence) that make you an *effect*. It can be more easily handled in *processing*—or you can simply let things "cool down" and come back to it again.

While it may seem "mysterious" to beginners, a *Seeker* gets a sense for knowing how long to *run* a *process* only with practice. Once you have spent some time actually applying the *Professional Course*, there are many aspects that become "second nature" because they are, in fact, a part of our true original nature. All we have done is "*reverse engineer*" the routes of *creation* and *consideration* that are already *our own*.

LESSON ONE: INCREASING AWARENESS

FIRST FLIGHTS ON THE PATHWAY

"*Processes*" are systematic techniques—or *actions*—that are repeated toward a specific *end-point* or result. In most cases, they consist of a repetitive instruction—or "*command-line*"—that is *run* over and over until something happens. This is what produces a *realization*, which may not happen the first few *runs*. The same idea applies to hammering a nail with multiple strikes rather than simply pushing hard against it.

The first lessons of the *Professional Course* are in some ways a review of many of the *techniques* introduced in the *Basic Course*. However, in this course, we will examine them much further as *processing* applications. In the *Basic Course*, just a few of the most critical *processes* are given as light *exercises* to supplement introductory lessons on the fundamental theory and philosophy of *Systemology*.

Much of the basic theory behind "*Systematic Processing*" may be found in *Lesson #6* of the *Basic Course*. In this *Professional Course*, we will be handling the *processes* directly as applications of our philosophy—and as a practical approach to unfolding the essential map of the *Pathway*, as researched by the *Systemology Society*.

SELF-DIRECTING ATTENTION

Consider for a moment that an *Alpha-Spirit* is able to *Self-direct* its nearly unlimited *Awareness*—and this has taken place across a long span of perceived existence (that we refer to as a *Spiritual Timeline*). Although the potential *Awareness* seems without limit, the ability to *handle* it has actually deteriorated over time, and with it, the potential "considerations" an *Alpha-Spirit* maintains of its own *Beingness*.

Understand that the original potential is *not* truly lost to us. It has, however, become *fragmented*. And by this, we mean that an individual's *attention* gets drawn toward painful instances and dangerous circumstances—and other "human problems" that can "fix" our *attention*. This, in fact, lowers the total *Awareness* immediately available to us; it affects just how much of our true *Self-determinism* is "in play."

Systematic Processing, in general, is an exercise in "*selectively directing attention.*" This is one of the reasons it is so effective for increasing *Awareness*. The exercises given in the *Basic Course*—particularly those related to "*presence in-session*" or the *Opening Procedures* for a *Formal Session* —are the most fundamental *processes* by themselves, because they "orient" a *Seeker* in present time and space to make any other *processing* workable.

Our *processing* methods are effective when they can collect (or concentrate) a *Seeker's* available *Awareness* (or "actualized" *Awareness*) and then increase it. This is essentially the *opposite* of hypnotism. In *processing*, a *Seeker* "frees up" more of their available "*attention units*" by taking them off of whatever they have been fixed on *unknowingly* throughout one's existence. These "*units*" have gotten stuck on things along the way.

"*Fragmentation*" is an archaic systemological term we still use today because it implies a "dispersal" of energy—or quite literally the "fracture" of a wholeness or totality into many parts. It is meant that some *thing* is in the way of a "clear view" (or "clear communication").

In most cases, *fragmentation* concerns what we don't want to *confront* directly—so we kind of "shut down" on those areas and withdraw, but without actually taking all of our *attention units* off of it. We don't really want to deal with it, but we can't trust it not to "bite" us when we're not looking. This "area" sinks into the shadowy gray parts of our *Awareness* until it becomes completely handled *unknowingly* "on automatic."

We have also retained the word "*imprint.*" This is best understood in this wise: you may have noticed that you are likely to give something more *attention* when it is first encountered—and certainly, common language makes frequent use of the phrase "*first impression.*" It is at these instances that we essentially take the data we have received and duplicate it as our own *Reality*. And this is what we agree to as *being Reality*.

When an *Alpha-Spirit* stops "*looking*" and "*creating,*" and starts using *imprinting* as the basis of *Reality*, the total available *Awareness* declines. The individual is still carrying the same amount of *Spiritual Awareness Energy* (or *ZU*) as they always have—but these energy stores have become increasingly "solidified." The heavier or more solid these energy units are, the farther below the line of *Actualized Awareness* they sink.

For *processing* to be effective, we begin with those *techniques* that will bring together those "*attention units*" that *are* actually accessible to a *Seeker*. These are also useful as general methods for "*selectively directing attention*" on other tasks, or in times of mental or emotional strain.

"Orientation in Present Space-Time" is also a critical part of the *Standard Opening Procedures* for a *Formal Session*.

The alternating *"command-lines"* in the sample script for a *Formal Session* are:

"Look around and spot something in the room."
"What do you notice about that?"

Of course, this is taken from a *"Traditional Piloting"* transcript, which involves two individuals—a *Pilot* and a *Seeker*—and is dependent on their relay of communication. Many variations of this are effective. An alternative *processing command-line* (or *"PCL"*) that may be more applicable for *"Solo-Processing"* (rather than the communicative approach), is:

"Look around and notice things. Locate precise points on the object, moving quickly from one point to another."

In basic terms, this *knowingly* duplicates the original basic systematic process of *imprinting*. This is what we do when we encounter a new person or enter a new place—at least *before* we tend to leave our ability to *perceive* and *create* (or *duplicate*) on automatic. We take a permanent "snapshot" to base our total *Reality*, but its vibrancy often fades. This is why the vividness of *Life* and the *Universe* can seem so "dull" sometimes.

Now, it is important when doing this *process* that you are actually "spotting precise points" with your full *attention* and not just casually glancing all about. Remember that these *are* "systematic processes" in spite of how plain the language used actually is, or how simple or trivial the action required may seem.

When using this *process* during periods of emotional turbulence or mental strain, you may suddenly feel more alert or clearer in your perceptions. Even if already awake and alert, there should be a sense of improvement, or perhaps the room may seem to be a little "brighter" than before. In either case, you would acknowledge (even to yourself, if *Flying-Solo*) that the *process* has reached a satisfactory "*end-point.*"

In addition to the improved "orientation in present space-time," this *process* also demonstrates the ability of the *Alpha-Spirit* to direct its *attention* and therefore control its experience of a mental state. Such is an example of a potential "*realization*" that might also spontaneously occur as a result of *running* this *process*.

ADVANCED APPLICATIONS

There are many applications for the previous *process* other than focusing *presence* for additional *processing*. In fact, early experiments with "*presence*" led to an entire route of advanced work (otherwise referred to as "A.T.") regarding *perception* of—and *operation* in—existence as an *Alpha-Spirit*, but independent of *any* body. Such is the *true* native state of *Self*.

This more advanced subject is presently brought up because of its ability to illustrate just how "not-trivial" the previous *process* really is. This became evident when *Seekers* assisting with research at the *Systemology Society* began to experiment with the previous *process*, but with their *eyes closed*.

Whether eyes are open or closed, this type of technique is called "*objective processing*" because it pertains directly to the "objective environment" or *Physical Universe* (*Beta-Existence*). This is quite different from a "*subjective process*" that calls for a *Seeker* to "remember" or "consider" something. There are other types, but the majority fall within either of these two categories.

If a *Seeker* wishes to experiment with the advanced version: start with the previous *process* as given while seated comfortably in a room. Once you have reached an *end-point* with that, close your eyes and repeat the *process* using an "imaginary" view of the room.

This practice is best done without straining and without concerns about accuracy. It is important, especially early on the *Pathway*, to acknowledge every "win" without invalidating a level of ability not yet regained. A *Seeker* should also avoid repeatedly opening their eyes to "check" whether or not their personal "copy" fits what is otherwise viewable with the body's eyes.

When first practicing with a technique like this, there are likely to be a lot of gaps of *real perception* filled-in with "created" or "imagined" scenery. Much of it will not necessarily be a one-to-one duplicate of what the body sees. It is also possible to perceive things that *are* "real," which the body is not able to sense.

Although presented early in our instructional lessons, this version is actually part of the advanced *processes* because its application is not restricted to standard "*defragmentation*" procedures. It is just one example of the *processing* we treat in this *Professional Course* that continues to be practiced at "advanced levels." It does not particularly have a "finite" *end-point* when applied during this lifetime.

Another application of this formula is to *knowingly* focus *attention* on specific points of the body (or *genetic-vehicle*). There is a tendency to operate the body on "auto-pilot." Often, our *attention* "snaps-in" on the body rather violently during painful incidents—and *then* we are suddenly *very aware* of it. The lack of *Self-determinism* involved in this abrupt shift in *Awareness* only reinforces the falsehood that we *are* our bodies.

HELPFUL TIPS ON PROCESSING

The second *process* we will introduce in the *Professional Course* is also an integral part of *Opening Procedures*. It is part of a cycle referred to as "Command of the Mind-Body Connection." Where we previously have *knowingly Self-directed* our *attention* to "spot" things, we now make deliberately intended actions to both "reach" and "withdraw" from them. This will also allow for additional training on general *processing*.

Perhaps one of the more challenging aspects for beginners to grasp about *processing*, is knowing just how long to *run* a *process* for. There is, of course, a liability to either *running* a *process* too long or not long enough.

For example: if a *process* is left as an incomplete cycle, a *Seeker* does not earn the gains or new *realizations* they otherwise would—and they likely have left a bit of *attention* on something stirred up, but not handled. On the other hand: if a *process* is run too long, a *Seeker* may start to feel tired (or "heavy")—the actual end-point when they felt better from the *process* was missed or unacknowledged.

There is much less liability—and by this, we mean the chance of hindrance of progress on the *Pathway*—by experimenting with *"overrun"* and *"underrun"* on these more fundamental *"objective processes."* Getting a "sense" for this early on the *Pathway* allows greater certainty in handling more intensive *processing* further along. This is of tremendous importance for *Seekers* intending to *Solo-Pilot* the entire *Professional Course*.

This *process* immediately follows the previous one in the *Standard Opening Procedures* of a *Formal Session* because it builds on the *presence* and *certainty* already established. In order to "touch" and "let go" of an object, a *Seeker* must first "spot" the object in present space-time. This may seem like only a slight increase or gradual incline in the "challenge" or "difficulty level" presented to a *Seeker* —and rightfully so. Much of the stable progress earned along the *Pathway* will be attained this way.

The repetitive alternating *"processing command-lines"* ("PCL") given in the sample script for a *Formal Session* are:

"(Choose an object.) Decide you are going to reach for it; then make that body pick it up."

"Now decide when you are going to put it down and make that body put it back where it was."

Usually, once a specific object is chosen, the *process* is *run* on that same item repetitively. While this example is quite direct, there are many PCL variations that could be just as effectively applied. What's given above is not even the most basic form of this *process*, which is:

"(Choose an object.) Decide on an exact spot on the object and reach for it."

"Now touch that spot for a moment; and then let go of it."

This is repeated over and over quite a few times. In addition to its use as a preliminary to a *Formal Session*, typically a *process* such as this is *run* in order for a *Seeker* to actually learn something, or come to a "new" *realization*. This is always our intention for *processing*; but in this case, it is to *realize* the level of "command" an individual directly has over the behaviors of their *Body* and functions of the *Mind*.

Putting the *realizations* of this specific *process* aside for a moment, let us use it to demonstrate *running* a *process* in general. For one thing: a continuing *Seeker* (from the *Basic Course*) with an understanding of the "*Beta-Awareness Scale*" (detailing a sequential range of emotions and mental states) may notice that an individual often comes *up* from the *bottom* of the scale during a *process*.

It requires a bit of *Self-determination* to get started on a *process* and quite a bit more to continue *running* it. In this example, it takes some time *running* to get past the immediate feeling of "*So what?*" or "*I touch things all the time.*" After further *running*, perhaps the attitude rises on the scale to "*This is stupid*" or "*This is boring.*" But if you push through this, a *Seeker* gets interested and starts to feel better and the object seems brighter. **This** is when you have reached an *end-point* on the *process*.

"*Underrun*" would be anything short of the *end-point* (such as the other states or attitudes just described). However, if you want to get a sense of "*overrun*," you can experiment with this same *process* by continuing it longer, past the appropriate *end-point* when you were feeling good about it. The longer you continue to *run* it, the further back down the *Beta-Awareness Scale* you may find yourself slipping; feeling worse about it and finding the repetition less tolerable and more difficult to handle than before.

Such *"overrun"* can easily take place during *processing*, when an *end-point* is not acknowledged (and the *process* is not stopped). In *"Traditional Piloting,"* it is up to an experienced practitioner to recognize these points—but when *Flying Solo*, a *Seeker* should get familiar with this phenomenon and know how to fix it.

The basic pattern observed of *overrun* is: a *process* begins "rough," then suddenly it "smooths" out and seems easy and fun (which is the *release-point* or *end-point*), and then it starts to feel "tough" again to continue doing. In this case, a *Pilot* has "flown past" or "bypassed" the appropriate "landing spot."

The most basic solution to *overrunning* a *process* is simply to "spot" the exact moment when you were feeling good and *did* reach an *end-point*. By "spot," we mean to definitively notice or perceive something distinctively—and not necessarily visually or with the eyes. If you can bring to mind the instance when you were feeling good about the object, then it should start to seem that way again.

At the other end of things, *"underrun"* is primarily a result of one's own premature *withdrawal* from the *process*. It only occurs by stopping a *process* before an *end-point* is reached. When not due to outside interruption, this usually happens when the content or data addressed by a *process* causes discomfort.

In the example we have been using, there is very little mental strain or emotional turbulence attached to touching and letting go of an object in our surroundings—unless perhaps we have selected an object that we don't particularly "*like*" very much. But in later *processes*, once something is critically stirred up, it is important not to *withdraw* from it simply because it seems "difficult."

The "difficulties" initially encountered with handling something "turbulent" are much different than how things seem when something is *overrun*. For one thing: if a *process* is *underrun*, a *release-point* or *end-point* has not yet been reached. So we don't want to *withdraw* from a *process* just because it feels uncomfortable.

Therefore, if something is "happening" (*e.g.*, there is movement on the *Awareness Scale*) or a *process* has "triggered" or "turned on" a reactive-mechanism, the only systematic action is to continue *running* the *process* until the *end-point* is actually arrived at. This is why we use "*sessions*" to avoid outside influence; because if the present *restimulation* is due to the *process*, then continuing to *run* that *process* will handle it. And, of course, the moment it is actually *handled*—when you "feel good" about it—you *end* the *process*.

TOUCH-AND-LET-GO

We use the "*touch-and-let-go*" exercise as a training example at the *Mardukite Academy*, but it is also a real *process*. The standard version has already been relayed:

"*Look around and choose an object.*"
"*Now, choose a specific spot on the object.*"
"*Touch and let go of it (until you feel good about it).*"
"*Choose a different spot on the object; and do the same.*"

"Do this on individual spots until the object seems more acceptable to you."

After having some practice with this *process* on many "spots" using various different objects, you can then apply this technique in everyday life with various things you find yourself using frequently. This is especially useful on "things at work"—and also on automobiles; everyone should be required to do this on vehicles before they are driven among other individuals.

As a variation of this (in *processing*), it is quite standard to have a *Seeker* "spotting spots" on "walls" of the *processing* room, and performing the same *"touch-and-let-go"* cycles. This not only increases personal *"presence"* (of *Awareness*) in present space-time, but also increases the vibrancy of the room. Using "walls" in this *process* enables directing *Awareness* on "spots" that are not part of objects or particularly interesting.

In a *Formal Session*, *"objective processing"* (such as this) is also applied in between the more "introspective" *processes*, in order to maintain a *Seeker*'s orientation (or *"presence"*) of *Awareness* (in present space-time). This is particularly important during prolonged *intensive sessions* that include many individual *processes*.

Advanced applications of this basic *"touch-and-let-go"* technique require "mentally reaching out" with *attention* —or extending/projecting one's *Awareness*—like a beam of energy.

As with handling the very first process given in this lesson, you would practice by beginning with the "physical" version (and *running* it to an *end-point*) and then switch over to the "mental" one (using the same object). This would first be *run* with eyes open: *looking* at the object and mentally reaching—not just with your *attention*, but as if you are actually making "contact" (or "touching") the object. It can also be *run* with eyes closed.

Another advanced variation of this is applied to the *Standard Opening Procedures* of a *Formal Session*, when a *Seeker* is directed to:

"Close your eyes. Put all of your attention on the upper two back corners of the room and just get real interested in them for a while."

WILLINGNESS TO REACH

One reason we practice deliberate (*Self-determined*) and repetitive *"touch-and-go"* cycles is because so much of this activity in our lives becomes "automated" and "reactive." For example: if we touch a "hot" surface, the reflex to pull away (retract or *withdraw*) is not *Self-determined*. This lack of *Self-determinism* even contributes to prolonging the sense of "pain" we may experience afterward.

One of the systematic techniques for handling this, which can be used in everyday life, is called the *"touch back."* By this, we mean duplicating the action that hurt you on your own *Self-determinism*. Of course, we mean to do this *slowly* and *safely*. This should include repetitive *"touch-and-go"* on various objects in the location of the incident, in addition to whatever caused the actual injury. But, for example: in the case of a "hot stove," you would wait until it cooled; or you would cover the edge of a "sharp" instrument, &tc.

The automation or reactivity of a "*flinch*" or "*withdrawal*" also involves a decrease in *Actualized Awareness*. It is simply inherent in the systematic mechanisms at work. When you are hurt, *attention* may "snap-in" on the body as an *effect*, but the actual *Self-determined Awareness* withdraws.

Even with emergency medical attention, the "withdrawal" or "avoidance" of *Self-determining attention* on that area will inhibit healing. Most physicians will agree that beyond the medical care they can provide, the rest is the patient's attitude.

For example: even with something as simple as "stubbing your toe"—you may have noticed that the sting of the pain continues to hurt after the incident takes place; and for a surprisingly long time, given the lack of real damage that usually occurs. What's more: there is a tendency to "stub" the same toe again soon afterward, because we have also *withdrawn* our attention from the toe and prefer not to *confront* the event.

The short answer to this "mystery"—and most aspects of *defragmentation* in general—is "*Awareness.*" An application of the "*touch back*" in the above example would be to *Self-determine* moving your foot slowly to lightly contact the surface you had hit.

The first time, the sharpness of the *restimulation* brings up to mind the original incident itself. But, after a few more *runs* of this *process*, the pain more quickly subsides (and there is less of a tendency for the same injury to repeat again). This is one example of applying *Systemology* philosophy to life that does not require a PCL or *"session"* to utilize—*although* specific instructions may be easily communicated if assisting another.

What we are starting to handle, in the long run, is the *"willingness to reach"*—and the more "physical" or "objective" exercises systematically *duplicate* the type of *mental processing* already taking place in the Mind. There is a tremendous amount of theory behind these techniques that is covered in the more advanced series of *Systemology Core* texts; but the *processes* given in this *Professional Course* speak volumes for themselves if properly applied.

THE WALL

The final *process* covered in this lesson is deceptively simple to *run*, and is also popularly spoken of by *Mardukite Academy* students. There is always a lot of gossip and jokes concerning *"The Wall."* This sometimes leads to not taking it seriously; but that is usually a result of not executing the actions in a fully *Self-determined* and precise manner. Each of the actions is made as if it is the *first time*; not simply a *repeat*.

The most basic PCL for this *process*:

"Look at that wall."
"Walk over to that wall."
"Touch the wall."
"Turn around."

This *process* is *run* in an open room between two walls. It is important that there is a clear path between the walls. It is preferable if the walls are bare. It is done *over* and *over* again. There is a point when *running* this *process* can really *"ping"* you with some discomfort; it may even stir up a lot of sensations that stem from things that remain "beneath the surface" and not yet accessible. But push through any of this and continue. Whatever point you start to feel good about handling control of the *Body*, end the *process*.

As with other examples of *"objective processing,"* this may also be applied as an advanced "eyes-closed" *process*. In this case it is best if you can lie down comfortably on the floor. And again, as with the other examples, you would begin your practice with the standard version, physically walking between the two walls. Afterward, you perform the same deliberate PCL actions, but *imagining* yourself as a *Spirit* doing it.

BETA-AWARENESS SCALE

4.0 SELF-HONESTY (BETA)
3.9 "Vibrant" ("Charismatic")
3.8 "Enthusiastic" ("In Love")
3.7 "Energetic"
3.6 "Cheerful"
3.5 CONFIDENT ("Positive")
3.4 "Determined"
3.3 "Eager"
3.2 "Alert" ("Attentive")
3.1 "Strong Interest"
3.0 INTERESTED ("Content")
2.9 "Small Interest"
2.8 "Encouraged"
2.7 "Disinterested"
2.6 "Doubtful"

2.5 INDIFFERENT ("Tolerant")
2.4 "Bored"
2.3 "Dislike" ("Neglectful")
2.2 "Tired"
2.1 "Monotony"
2.0 INVALIDATING ("Pessimistic")
1.9 "Antagonism"
1.8 "Suffering" ("In Pain")
1.7 "Confrontational"
1.6 "Violent"
1.5 ANGRY ("Negative")
1.4 "Hateful"
1.3 "Spiteful"
1.2 "Resentment"
1.1 "Anxiety"
1.0 FEAR ("Afraid")
0.9 "Terror"
0.8 "Numb"
0.7 "Evasive"
0.6 "Loss"
0.5 GRIEF ("Sadness")
0.4 "Depression"
0.3 "Victimization"
0.2 "Hopelessness"
0.1 "Apathy" ("Unconsciousness")
0.0 BETA CONTINUITY (Organic Death)

THE FORMAL SESSION (EXAMPLE SCRIPT)

1. BEGINNING THE SESSION

"Would it be okay with you if we begin this session now?"

"Okay."

"Start of session."

2. OPENING PROCEDURES

A. Presence In-Session

"Is there anything going on that might keep your attention from being present in-session?"

(if *"no,"* acknowledge and go to *B.*; if *"yes,"* continue below)

"Okay. Tell me about it."

"Alright. How does that problem seem to you now?"

(if *"further away"* or handled, acknowledge and go to *B.*; if *"closer"* or more turbulent, continue below)

"Spot something in the incident; Spot something in the room."

(this alternating command line is repeated as needed)

B. Orientation in Present Space-Time

"Get the sense of you making that body sit in that chair."

"Okay. Get a sense of the floor beneath your feet."

"Do you have that real good?"

(if *"no,"* acknowledge and repeat *A.*; if *"yes,"* continue below)

"Recall a time something seemed real to you."

"Tell me something you notice about it."

"Look around and spot something in the room."

"What do you notice about that?"

(these last four command lines are repeated in series as needed; acknowledge and continue below)

C. Control of Body and Mind In-Session

(two dissimilar objects—here given as *"Item-1"* and *"Item-2"*—are presented and placed within reach; or alternatively, at two distant points in the room, in which a command line for "walking" between them would be inserted)

"Pick up Item-1."

"Tell me about its weight."

"Tell me about its color."

"Tell me about its texture."

"Put it down."

"Pick up Item-2."

"Tell me about its weight."

"Tell me about its color."

"Tell me about its texture."

"Put it down."

(this series of command-lines may be repeated several times; when there is no communication-lag for several full series, and duplicate answers are reoccurring, acknowledge and continue below)

"Choose an object. Decide when you are going to reach for it. Then make that body pick it up."

"Now decide when you are going to put it down. Then make that body put it back where it was."

(repeat as needed; when there is no communication-lag for a full series of command lines, acknowledge and continue below)

"Close your eyes. Put all of your attention on the upper two back corners of the room and just get real interested in them for a while."

(if there are no visible signs of "strain" after two minutes, acknowledge and continue below)

D. Establishing the Session

"Do you have any goals for this session, or anything in particular you want to address?"

(acknowledge, then start a process)

3. STARTING A PROCESS

"I would like to start a process; would that be okay?"

"Alright. The command lines are ---. Does this make sense?"

(if *"no,"* clear up any misunderstood words; if *"yes,"* start the process)

4. CHANGING A PROCESS

(only the wording in a command line may be changed to make it more workable for a *Seeker*; to change processes altogether, the present process must reach an end-point)

Example: a Seeker expresses inability to "imagine" or visualize imagery.

"Okay. Well, just 'get a sense' of..." or *"Just 'get the idea' of..."*

Example: a Seeker expresses discomfort (or withdrawal from) recalling a particular incident.

"That's fine. What part of that incident 'could' you confront?"

5. STOPPING A PROCESS

(when an end-point has been reached on a repetitive-style process)

"We'll just run this process a couple more times if that's okay with you?"

(general process is run two more times)

"Okay. Is there anything you would like to tell me before we end this process?"

(**or**, if an end-point "realization" is communicated from a process)

"Alright. Very good."

(the formal end of a particular process requires a command-line)

"End of process."

6. ENDING THE SESSION

(once a process, or series of processes, is completed)

"Is there anything you would like to tell me before we end this session?"

(if *"yes,"* acknowledge and handle it with communication before ending the session; if *"no,"* continue below)

"Would it be okay if we ended this session now?"

"Okay."

"End of session."

LESSON TWO: THOUGHT & EMOTION

KEEPING A FLIGHT LOG

Whether a *Seeker* is *Co-Piloted* or *Flying-Solo*, it is traditional to keep a *"Flight Log"* or *record* of the journey on the *Pathway*. This follows in line with the systematic approach of our philosophy. It is also helpful to refer to if running into any misunderstood *turbulence* along the way—such as *"underrun"* or *"overrun"* of a *process*, as described in the first lesson of this *Professional Course*.

A *Systemologist* keeps careful records of their *"processing sessions"* and any other *realizations* that have occurred while traveling the *Pathway*. In 2020, the *Systemology Society* developed the *"Truth Seeker's Adventure Journal"* to make this easier—but you can easily use any notebook to "log" your progress if you know what information is most critical to keep track of. Be consistent.

The following is a brief list of all general information tracked in *Traditional Piloting*:

–*Name* of the *Pilot* or *Co-Pilot*;
–*Location* and *Weather*;
–*Date* and *Day of the Week*;
–*Beta-Awareness* (at *start/end* of session);
–*Time* (at *start* and *end* of session);
–*Processes*, *Routines* or *Procedures* used;
–*Terminals* (*masses, objects, people, places*)
  contacted/recalled/imagined in session;
–Everything a *Seeker says* in session; and
–Any *Realizations* that occur.

Records are important for optimum effectiveness and tracing any incomplete *processes* or other sources of *turb-*

ulence that may have become accessible, where they were not before. The techniques included in the *Professional Course* series are not meant to be particularly strenuous, however, even the most basic of these *processes* can "stir up" or "trigger" various things—each of which should be handled as they *resurface*.

Another purpose for *journaling* as a standard routine is to "*extrovert*" after a session; to get all the stuff that took place down on paper, externally. This also helps keep a *Seeker* from keeping any residual attention remaining on the session and not in present space-time once the session has ended.

CONTROL OF MIND AND BODY

Thoughts (of the "*Mind*") and subsequent *emotions* (of the "*Body*") are under the command of the *Alpha-Spirit*. Of course, we often find ourselves relinquishing the control of these aspects to others. Sometimes it is simply a part of the roles we play—or perhaps it helps to keep things interesting—but in the end, it is always within your power to regain total control of your *thoughts* and *emotions*.

Some basic exercises in this area of "attitude control" are provided in the *Basic Course*, as is an introduction to the *Beta-Awareness Scale*. However, let us start off this lesson with a demonstration of light "*objective processing*."

"*Choose a 'neutral' object (that you have no strong feelings about).*"

"*Look at the object.*"

"*Decide to feel various positive things about the object (that you love it, that it is beautiful to look at, that it is wonderful to have close to you, &tc)."*

"Maintain this positive attitude for several minutes."

"(Then reverse this and) Decide to feel various negative things about the object (that you despise it, that it is ugly to look at, that it is harmful to be near, &tc) and continue this for several minutes."

"(Then reverse this again and) Decide to maintain a positive attitude about the object for several minutes."

When this *process* is practiced seriously, a *Seeker* may initially encounter some challenges in exercising their fluid alternation of attitudes back and forth. Various unintended "reactions" may also occur as one makes the decision to feel one way or another. This should be repeated several times on the same object until any automatic reaction or turbulence has "smoothed out"—or *"flattened"* as we tend to say (using *wave* terms).

Once this has been *run* and *flattened* on the same object, you may then use the *process* again on other objects in the room. Always end-off during the "positive" side of an alternating *process*, rather than the "negative." This *process* is not intended to solve all *fragmentation* preventing total control of the *Mind* and *Body*; but it is a very productive practice—and it may lead to the same *realizations* on which our theories for it are based.

ASSOCIATIVE IDENTIFICATION

Much of what *Humans* consider as *"knowledge"* really relates to *"associative identification"*—or more simply, *"association."* Entire fields of philosophy—such as *"epistemo-*

logy"—are dedicated to theories to explain "*how* we *know* what we *know.*" *Systematic Processing* allows a *Seeker* a direct approach to determining the truth of these matters for themselves.

Early work by the *Mardukite Research Org* served as a precursor to establishing the *Systemology Society*—and within that body of early research, we uncovered a significant amount of information regarding the control of human consciousness with "*language*" at the inception of modern civilization thousands of years ago.

Most "*thinking*" involves *association*, not *Knowingness*. The type of *realizations* that occur in *processing* lead to a higher state of actual *Knowingness*. This *Knowingness* is not the result of freewheeling thought—it is not a result of "thinking about" or "figuring on" things. The systematic approach we take in *processing* is similar to natural "thought processes"—but a *Seeker* more directly is applying *attention* to actually *look* at things.

The following *process* demonstrates all of these points. When first practicing this, it is most effective to select an object present around you that has a lot of "mass" to it—such as a table, a chair, or a bookshelf, *&tc.* Then, select something else with "mass" (not present in the environment) that it would be ridiculous to associate with the object—such as an apple, a garden-hose, or a stop-sign, *&tc.*

The basic "*processing command-line*" (or "PCL") for this exercise is:

"*Look at the object and immediately think of the ridiculous association you have chosen.*"

　–or–

"Look at the object and think of the ridiculous association as if it were automatic."

To be most effective, it is best if you alternate doing this with *looking* at something else around you and noticing something about it. Then you can redirect your *attention* back to the object you are working with, and getting an immediate sense that it is the ridiculous alternative association instead.

As an advanced application, you might try to actually *imagine* or *visualize* the intended alternative in place of the object. When you "spot" this *imagined* alternative, make a point to *notice* specific things about it. This will also increase the detail or vibrancy of your *visualization.* This may be practiced further using various different objects in your environment and associating other alternative ridiculous items.

Usually we *associate* "ideas" and "concepts" in our "*thinkingness,*" but the actual substance or significance we attach to our thoughts and feelings often regards something with "mass"—which is to say, a "*terminal*" using *Systemology* vocabulary. We treat specific *terminals* more directly in later "*subjective processes.*"

CREATING EMOTIONAL FLOWS

Strength and ability of an *Alpha-Spirit* is rooted in *Self-determinism*—of being *at cause*. Therefore, we find that misappropriating (or inappropriately assigning) *cause* in our life is one of the many ways in which we increasingly come to consider ourselves primarily the *effect* of others, and even the *Universe* as a whole.

It is quite customary with the *Human Condition* to assign *cause* of "ill effects" as far away from *Self* as possible. From this, we tend to "blame" others for how we think and feel. This is not to say there are not many influential factors to our experiences; but ultimately, it is *Self* that decides how to think and feel.

Whenever we "incite" or "inspire" an *emotional reaction* in another, they sometimes tell us that we *caused* them to *feel* this or that way—that *they* are experiencing the *effect* of our *presence*. Of course, many factors are likely at play here; but the ability to *create* a specific *emotion, sensation* or state of *thought* is certainly within the power of an *Alpha-Spirit*.

With *objective processing*, a *Seeker* can *knowingly* practice getting this sense of *creating* or *projecting* an "*emotional flow.*" This will also start to familiarize a *Seeker* with the idea of more directly considering (or treating) all *energy, communication* and *attention-lines* as a "*flow.*"

"*Look around and choose an object.*"

"*(Alternate) Make it feel happy; Make it feel sad.*"

When practicing this, perform the action by *intention*. You don't need to actually "say" anything—telling jokes or scolding—to produce the effect. Just get the sense of deciding upon, and intending, the idea or concept very strongly and clearly. Then, get the sense that just being in your presence makes it happen.

After this is practiced for a while on a specific object, try it on other items in the room. Once you are comfortable with this pair of states, consider other states on the *Beta-Awareness Scale* such as "*love*" and "*hate*"; then with "*interest*" and "*boredom.*" Starting with the extremes will eventually allow you to easily practice with any emotion or mental state.

When we interact with the *Universe*—and other lifeforms in the *Universe*—*communications* "*flow*" in various directions between *terminals*. In *Systemology*, we refer to these individual *flows* as "*circuits*"—therefore "*circuits*" between "*terminals*." We adopted this terminology from the field of electronics; but, this systematic approach has allowed us to understand and apply our philosophy in *systematic processing*.

"Look around and choose an object."
"(Alternate) Get a sense of feeling sorry for the object; get a sense of the object feeling sorry for you."

Practice for a while on the same object, then pick another item and do the same. If a *Seeker* continues this long enough, the ultimate *end-point* would be a greater control over the *reactivity* associated with "*grief*" and "*sympathy*." A complete mastery is not expected with a single pass through the *Professional Course*.

This *process* may be applied to other states of *Beta-Awareness*—"fear" or "*being afraid of*"; "anger" or "*being angry at*"; "cheerfulness" or "*happy to have you/it there*"; &tc. Again, working with these states *knowingly* in *processing* should produce some sense of having a greater control over the experience of them.

AUTOMATION AND REACTIVITY

One of the principle areas of *Systemology* is the study of *automated mechanisms* and *reactivity*. In basic terms: this is how *systems* influence one another. Most systems are *dynamic*, which means that they do not exist in exclusion separately from other *systems*; thus their *"state"* may be influenced by other outside *"conditions."*

The *Alpha-Spirit* has the ability to command the control of all its *systems*—and the ability to automate that control as well. While the *"Body"* does receive its commands from various Mind-Systems, much of what is handled by the *"Mind"* takes place on *automatic*, leading *unknowingly* to act out behaviors as a *reaction*.

A systematic way of handling those tendencies of the *Human Condition* that are happening on *automatic* is to *knowingly* "exaggerate" their behavior. This is far easier than invalidating early efforts to "stop" it altogether at first. Then, in practice, you alternate doing it more and doing it less. You basically keep doing the thing *knowingly* until it seems to come more under your control.

There are many aspects of the *Human Condition* that are experienced *"on automatic,"* but this basic technique is quite effective for handling the most accessible (visible or already known) tendencies. Let's try another exercise within the same area of *processing*.

"Close your eyes."

"What are you looking at?"

Some individuals see a specific *mental image* (*visual picture*), or *energy-bursts*, or even *blackness* (but a uniquely intense *blackness*) when they close their eyes. This occurs seemingly automatically. The *process* continues:

"Make a duplicate copy of what you see (right next to it)."

However a *Seeker* manages this action is acceptable. It

might be an *imagined* "holographic" duplicate; or perhaps you imagined a "screen" (as a background) to place a copy on. At first, we are really only concerned with getting a sense of this, even if the *Seeker* has difficulty with creating vivid *mental images*.

Once a single copy of whatever is seen is made next to it, make another duplicate copy on the other side. Now make more copies to the right and to the left. Don't limit the space to a linear horizon in front of you; make more copies above your head and below your feet and behind you. Then continue to the next *process*.

"Close your eyes."
"What are you looking at?"
"Make a mental image copy of it."
"Now change its color; Turn it ---."

Whatever the color-quality already (or *automatically*) is, *"turn it..."* to another color. In between cycles of this *process*, be sure to open your eyes and look around your environment, spot things and notice specific points on them. This alternates using purely "mental" exercises with reorienting *presence* in that space and time. As an advanced application, a *Seeker* creates many copies and starts changing the color of each one individually.

We have mentioned *"association"* previously in this lesson; a large amount of our *associated knowledge* is made up of "automatic" and "reactive" *mental imagery* that represents the *"terminal"* or "mass" that we *most "associate"* with that concept or piece of data. Often, this restricts us from considering a wider scope (or range) of potential possibilities.

There is another phenomenon observed in *Systemology*,

referred to as a *"compulsively created mental image."* This is otherwise called a *"stuck picture"*—one that is consistently brought to mind, or *unknowingly created*, outside of, or without, one's own *Self-determinism*. Most individuals have a few of these that are *imprints* of incidents and past experiences. More often then not, a *"stuck picture"* is of something unpleasant.

For example: if you are worried about something, there is often a *"mental image"* representing whatever you are worried about that is *"stuck in your mind"*—which is to say, that you can't stop thinking about. The systematic solution is to make many copies of the *"stuck picture"*— first changing its color, then altering the entire nature of the imagery one part at a time until the whole "scenery" comes under your control.

"Look around (the room) and spot an object."
"What thought comes to mind?"
"Make a duplicate copy of the thought."
"Make another copy (make many copies, thinking it many times)."
"(Alternate) Make the thought 'louder'; Make the thought 'quieter'."

Having the nature and intensity of thoughts under your control will assist in better handling those aspects and items we'd rather not *confront*.

CONFRONTING "AS-IT-IS"

The word *"confront"* has many negative connotations in modern language. For example, we tend to refer to someone who is quick to exhibit anger with others as *confrontational*. But this only partly demonstrates the true meaning of the word, which is: "to come around to the front"—or "come around to face."

In some ways, we have been lightly (but directly) "*confronting*" objects, emotions, and states of mind throughout this lesson. We have demonstrated that control over our experience of something, lies not in our avoidance or withdrawal, but our willingness to *look* at it "*As-It-Is*."

The first basic *confront processes* (also known as "*concentering*" in archaic "*New Thought*" traditions) are important, but easily dismissed or incorrectly performed. The ability to properly *confront* existence "*As-It-Is*"—and free of automatic-associations and other reactivity—is a critical component to the *Pathway*. But, this does not take place all at once, just as the "blockage" to this native ability did not always seem as solid.

When we *look* at something "*As-It-Is*," we are *confronting* it. The ability to do this in *Self-Honesty*—without those *associations* and *reactivity*—is a practiced skill, one that improves the further along the *Pathway* one progresses.

Not unlike states sought through traditional forms of "*meditation*," to *confront*, we practice by simply *looking* at something with all of our *presence* and *attention* without any *distraction*—either from the "*Body*," the environment, or thoughts. This also increases personal ability to provide *presence* and focus *attention*.

There is an archaic *Tibetan* tradition of "*Sitting Face-to-Face*" which a *Seeker* may practice best with a partner. This is performed by simply sitting across from another person without talking or giving in to reactions. In *sess-*

ion, this may be practiced with an object. What is important is to be able to "extrovert" your *attention;* to project it to a point that is outside and away from where you *perceive* the *"Body"* or *"Mind"* to be located.

Unlike the previous *process*—where we "make a copy" of distractions (thoughts and emotions) to practice getting them under our control—this exercise is not concerned with addressing each distraction as a *thing,* but rather ignoring them and refocusing *attention* exactly where you want it. Much may "stir up" in the *"Body"* and *"Mind"* just by sitting quietly maintaining eye contact with someone.

If any discomfort, emotional reactions or intruding thoughts "stir up" or "turn on" while performing this *process,* simply maintain focus of your *attention* "outwards" until they "simmer down" or "turn off." There are many times in *Life* when you need to persist or handle something in spite of distractions, and the ability to do this *clearly* without losing *focus,* is an important skill for optimum *survival* (and our ability to *create*).

This may be practiced until you are able to achieve these results effortlessly for a few minutes at will. Afterward, reapplying the *"Control of Mind-Body" process* used in the *"Opening Procedures"* of a *Formal Session* (and reintroduced in *Lesson-1* of this series) may yield different results. The PCL for this is:

"Put all of your attention on the upper back corners of the room; Keep your attention there and ignore all distractions."

INTRODUCING SUBJECTIVE PROCESSING

The sequential *Pathway to Ascension* relayed in this *Professional Course* series of lessons begins with a lot of "*objective universe processing.*" This means those *processes* which mainly "extrovert" *attention*, or focus it "*external*" to the "*Body*" on the "objective" *Universe*. Even when treating something "*internal*" (like emotion and thought), we have, up until now, *processed* a "*projection*" of it into "*external*" objects.

The majority of *processing* used on the *Pathway* concerns the "*subjective universe*" of the individual themselves. This might be best understood as a *Seeker's* own "*Personal Universe.*" However, all of the previous *processes* allow for early personal development, are excellent demonstrations of *Systemology*, and quite useful for realigning full *presence* in between long periods of "introverted" *subjective processing*.

Conceptual Processing is a form of *subjective-universe processing* because it asks a *Seeker* to "consider," "conceive," or "get the sense of" a concept being (or not being) a certain way, in spite of how it might really appear or manifest in this *objective-universe* (that is otherwise agreed to as "*Reality*" for all concerned).

Since *subjective-universe processing* is such an integral part of the remaining *Professional Course* series, it is important that we introduce it, and its systematic application, in the earliest lessons. There is also some additional instruction that is necessary, which a *Seeker* should combine with what they've already learned about *systematic processing* in general. This is important for *Flying-Solo* without experienced assistance.

Systematic Processing is *not* a form of meditation or psychotherapy; and it most certainly *isn't* freewheeling thought, where an individual just skips from one thought to another or lingers compulsively on one. Our methods originally developed from a need within the *Mardukite Research Organization* to provide *Seekers* with an effective form of ministerial counseling or spiritual advisement. *Systemology* developed thereafter.

When *Solo-Processing*, it does not help to start "spinning in" on endless cycles of *"thinkingness"* that ultimately leave you more confused, or at the very least, less certain, of your ability and your progress on the *Pathway*. It is *certainty*, and the brighter "feel good" *objective processes*, that will help carry you through the rough spots.

To avoid stimulating anything significant, we will introduce *subjective processing* with a "neutral" example that would not otherwise appear in a *session* and should not have any mental *"charge"* or emotional turbulence attached to it.

A *Pilot* gives (or a *Seeker* reads) the PCL: *"Think of a Fruit."* Now, the *Seeker* would either communicate (or write down) all the *"answers"* that come to mind from this. The two-way communication (or writing, if *Solo*) assists in keeping a *Seeker* from getting too introverted or "spun-in" on a *subjective process*.

At first, in this example, a *Seeker* might have to orient themselves, or internally *process* the *command-line* for a moment, and then the initial *"answer"* (or *"response"* to the mental inquiry) might be "a cherry." And so, this would be communicated (or written) the moment it comes into mind. This also allows that cycle to get acknowledged, and the *Seeker* is free to come up with another *answer*. Soon, many of them start to occur quite easily. The *end-point* here is when you feel good about *"thinking of fruits."*

If this were a *process* regarding something with *fragmentation* attached to it, there would initially be some noticeable difficulty or resistance in *running* the PCL—or the *"answers"* wouldn't make sense, or would be about something else. *Systematic Processing* increases a *Seekers "certainty"* in being able to push through the "mental barriers" and regain control of "emotional turbulence."

An example of *fragmentation* if *processing* our example, would include "spinning-in" on freewheeling-thought that concerns the nature, or definition, of what a *"fruit"* is, *&tc*. This is one of the reasons an experienced *Pilot* will make certain that a *Seeker* fully understands the words used in a PCL before using it in *processing*.

"Freewheeling thought" is what takes place due to *associations* and unfocused *attention*. For example: a *Seeker* answers (or writes) "a cherry" and then starts (internally) asking themselves questions about "cherry-pies," which leads to wondering if they are hungry, and so on. This is not *processing*. This does nothing to *flatten* the *"wave," "charge"* (or *"turbulence"*) of the *fragmentation* presenting itself.

When *running* a *process*, you want to focus on getting direct *responses* or *answers* to the PCL; even if it's not posed as a "question" outright. This is what makes our work a *systematic process*; because you are *looking* at *responses* or *answers* from a "computational databank." These are not random *responses*, but *answers* that result from *systematic processing* taking place "internally" in the "*Mind*" due to *running* our intended PCL.

During a *process*, the PCL is the query or question, which already puts a *Seeker* in some degree of *uncertainty*. The key to *running* a *process* is to then produce *responses* or *answers*, not pose more questions to yourself. If you consider each PCL in a "*What is..?*" form, you should be most focused on "*It is...*" answers.

BASIC SUBJECTIVE PROCESSING

To further illustrate the application and proper *running* of *subjective processing*, we will begin with a few light examples that are real *processes*. Alternating *command-lines* may be designated "A" and "B" (or however many steps there are to the *process*. These can be *logged* in a journal simply by putting the letters at the top of the page and using each subsequent line to keep track of the appropriate list. Therefore:

A. "*Think of something you wouldn't mind remembering. (What is it?)*"

B. "*Think of something you wouldn't mind forgetting. (What is it?)*"

This is systematically more effective than simply drilling on one consideration repeatedly. A *process* is already *run* in repetition, but doing this with *subjective processing* also allows you to realign your focus and avoid getting "spun-in" or "off-track" on some additional cycle of thought.

There are also *subjective processes* where you do simply keep listing *"answers"* from one PCL until one seems right—but that is only used when you are scouting for a specific *"answer"* and not unraveling a whole chain of *considerations*. This type of work will be treated later on in the *Professional Course* series.

In *running* our present example, you may find that answers do not immediately present themselves, but eventually they do—and at one point, perhaps quite quickly. There will then be a point when new answers don't seem to be occurring and suddenly the *process* seems difficult. The *realization* or improvement will usually come by pushing through this at least once, *looking* a bit "deeper" to see if there is something else.

"What is something you agree with?"
"What is something you disagree with?"

Using *subjective processing* for *defragmentation* generally consists of "freeing up" *considerations* that may otherwise be rigidly fixed in place as they are. This rigidity or solidity produces what we may refer to as a *"stuck flow"*—which is fixed continuously in one direction.

The systematic solution to this is to practice an *alternation* of *consideration* from multiple sides or angles. Without understanding this, some of our *processing* would be seen as counter-intuitive. For example:

"Decide that something is important."
"Decide that something is unimportant."

In *running* this, we aren't as much concerned with what that "something" is for a single *process*, or what the *Seeker* ultimately feels about it. The entire purpose is to practice *considering* that something *is* or *isn't*. As a result, an individual is more certain in their ability to actually "change their minds" of their own choosing.

For the final example in this section, separate your journal page into four columns—A, B, C, and D—and just think about something related to the categories given for each PCL. For each PCL, you will think about something and then list what *"it is"* as if responding to the follow up query of *"What is it?"* The answers are not as important as the practice of maintaining *Self-determined* control over your thoughts.

A. *"Think about Space."*
B. *"Think about Time."*
C. *"Think about Energy."*
D. *"Think about Matter."*

CONFRONTING THE PAST

Most of the *processing* presented in the *Professional Course* series will target specific areas. This is important for learning the various *processes* and *techniques*, and also for developing *certainty* and increased *Awareness* for when a *Seeker* cycles through the material of the entire course additional times.

Stable progress on the *Pathway*—and *processing sessions* in general—results from being able to handle (or *process*) whatever presents itself. A *Seeker* learns to *confront* rather than *withdraw* from their own *Mind*. But before that can happen, it is necessary to have *certainty* on the right *processes* to apply to the right situation.

Fragmentation is an accumulation of debris or blockage that occurs gradually over time. As our spiritual philosophy relays, the individual (or *Seeker*) as an *Alpha-Spirit* has been around for a very long time. It has followed its own path of existence as an *Awareness* that we refer to as a "*Spiritual Timeline.*"

The *Spiritual Timeline* extends like a "track"—and it includes all of our "*past*" existences (as an *Awareness*) far and beyond *this* physical incarnation (lifetime), or even *this* Universe. We presume that it extends well afterward into what we would consider the *future* as well. The part which is "*past*," we call the "*Backtrack.*"

We have mentioned "*stuck pictures*" and "*stuck flows*" or other rigidly fixed forms of *fragmentation* that limit our total potential and range of *considerations*. These actually accumulate as "energetic-masses" on our *Backtrack*. We often refer to these masses as "*imprints*" when they are *associated* with a specific *incident* or *terminal*. The more *imprints* accumulate, the more *fragmented* the experience of *Life* and *Existence* becomes.

Eventually, to fully *Self-Actualize* for *Ascension*, an individual needs to *clear* the channels of *fragmentation*, particularly those that include "*past trauma.*" If *Flying-Solo*, the best course of action is not to simply *fly* headlong straight into the trauma, but instead, to first build up *certainty* and *inertia* (or else, personal *horsepower*) with the basic *processes*—and *recalling* pleasant times to balance-out handling of the unpleasant.

To conceptualize the *Backtrack*, think of a long reel of "movie film" that is systematically categorized with various dates and incidents—along with the *considerations* that we made as a result of those events. An individual

(*Alpha-Spirit*) is as well off as they have full *Awareness* on the contents of their own *Backtrack*.

Those energetic-masses that accumulate actually block our clear view of the *Spiritual Timeline* or *Backtrack* and inhibit us from experiencing and handling better recall of the data. Although *attention units* of our *Awareness* are entangled up in the compulsive unknowing creation of these *imprints*, our resistance to wanting to *look* at them eventually turns into automatic tendencies that provide us only "*blackness*" to see.

Obviously, our existence has not only consisted of unpleasant experiences—and it is on these that we should put our attention in order to reduce any "*blackness*" that is associated with our history, in this lifetime or otherwise. When *Flying-Solo* without assistance of an experienced *Pilot* (or *Co-Pilot*), *u*se *recall* of "pleasant memories" if handling past trauma suddenly becomes too overwhelming.

There is the occasional phenomenon where a PCL directed at pleasure moments will instead trigger associated thoughts of loss, *&tc*. Although a *Seeker* doesn't want to get into a habit of *withdrawing* from such *reactivity* without handling it, the *process* only works by completing the PCL, and not diverting *attention* each time a *distraction* arises. We have practiced this already. If it happens, simply acknowledge that it exists and take it up in a later *process* or *session*.

ANALYTICAL RECALL

"*Analytical Recall*" processing is one of the first methods developed for applying our philosophy. At first, a *Seeker* needs only to *recall* or "remember" some aspect that the PCL calls for and then notice something about it.

As a *Seeker* becomes more experienced with *subjective processing* they will be in the habit of spotting various *"facets"* of a memory with these *processes*. These *facets* might include: time of day; location; living things present; emotions felt; any data sensed, such as smells, the quality of light, humidity—the list goes on.

There are four *processes* below. Each *process* consists of three PCL. These are *run* repetitively as an alternating cycle (1, 2, 3, 1, 2, 3...) until you feel good about doing the *process*. Then end the *session,* or go to the next *process.* When first practicing, focus on just spotting specific "times" and "people" (and any *terminals* of significant *"mass,"* such as a building, *&tc*).

Communication:
1. *"Remember a time when you enjoyed talking to someone."*
2. *"Remember a time when someone enjoyed talking to you."*
3. *"Remember a time when you saw two people enjoy talking to each other."*

Agreement:
1. *"Remember a time when you agreed with someone."*
2. *"Remember a time when someone agreed with you."*
3. *"Remember a time when you saw two people agree with each other."*

Liking:
1. *"Remember a time when you liked someone."*
2. *"Remember a time when someone liked you."*

3. *"Remember a time when you saw two people like each other."*

Understanding:

1. *"Remember a time when you felt that you really understood someone."*

2. *"Remember a time when you felt that someone really understood you."*

3. *"Remember a time when you felt two other people really understood each other."*

LESSON THREE: CLEAR COMMUNICATION

WILLINGNESS TO REACH FURTHER

Stable progress on the *Pathway-to-Ascension* is marked by states of increased *"Knowingness."* By this, we mean what a person *actually knows*. This *Knowingness* is quite different from what we are *told*, or other *associative knowledge*. We mean specifically: what a person already *knows* about *Self*, their *past*, *Life*, and all *Existence*—but, for whatever reasons, has *"blocked out"* from their present *Awareness*.

The long-run of the *Pathway-to-Ascension* is intended to return to an individual the *certainty* and *Knowingness* of their original native *"god-like"* state as an immortal *Alpha-Spirit*. We do not expect this to happen all at once; and there are many safe-guards of the Mind-System that prevent the flood-gates of total *Knowingness* from overwhelmingly *"caving-in"* on the *Seeker* all at once.

Spiritual fragmentation (which also includes matters of emotion and thought) accumulates beneath the surface of what an individual is presently *aware* of. Some use the words "unconscious" or "subconscious"—but these are not truly *systematic* terms. Yet, we do mean what is happening *unknowingly*.

Previously, in *Lesson #2* of this *Professional Course*, we introduced the idea of a continuous *"Spiritual Timeline,"* a "memory" that the individual carries of their eternal existence as an *Alpha-Spirit*. This includes the experience of *this* incarnation or "lifetime" as well as all others.

Having the entire memory of one's past—or *Backtrack* —*"resurface"* on them in one flash instant would be too overwhelming to behold. But it can safely occur gradually—and *Systematic Processing* is intended to help gradually restore *Knowingness* of the full basic state or *identity* of the individual as a *Spiritual Being*.

Of course, to accomplish these goals, one of the first requirements is that a *Seeker* actually be *"Willing to Know."*

In the previous *"Fundamentals of Systemology" Basic Course* series, we described the totality of *Awareness* as a "spectrum" divided into two main areas: what is clearly *known* and a dark area that is *not-known*. The dividing line between forms the basis for what is considered *"above"* or *"below"* the *"surface"* of *thought*.

This "line" is really a philosophical construct; so we aren't trying to move the "line." In *processing*, however, we are working to shift more of the *data* from the area of *"not-known"* to the area of *"known."* There is also a "gray area" of what is *almost-known*; what is *accessible* to a *Seeker* but remains *just* "beneath the surface."

The greater the *Willingness-to-Know*, and the more that is within an individual's *tolerance* to reach for, the "wider" or "larger" this *gray area* will be for what is *accessible* in *processing*. *Systematic Processing* both *accesses* what is *accessible* and increases the individual's *tolerance* to *confront* addition layers beneath it.

Fragmentation is handled as a series of layers—each layer representing a level of blockage. We don't usually make stable gains by simply digging a deep hole to what is buried far beneath. Too much of what surrounds at each layer will "cave-in" on the *Seeker*. Therefore, we strip away the debris in layers to expose the entire area underneath.

We have introduced the fundamentals of *systematic pro-*

cessing—specifically *subjective-universe processing*—in the previous lessons of this *Professional Course*. Included with this is advice and tips for handling *processes* as a *Solo-Pilot*, and a few maneuvers for getting yourself out of trouble if you encounter turbulence. With that in mind, let's start this lesson off with some light *processing*.

[Note: if you have already attained the ultimate *realizations* as *end-points* for any particular area (from a previous pass through this course material), then your practical instruction is to *"spot"* the moment it happened.]

EXPANDING WILLINGNESS

For *processes* like these, you want to *run* through as many cycles of the *"processing command-lines"* ("PCL") as you can, rather than dwelling on each individual answer. You want to generate a response as if it were an item on a list, then go to the next, rather than free-wheeling into an entire narrative or explanation.

Each *process* that follows here will consist of three PCL. These are *run* repetitively as an alternating cycle (1, 2, 3, 1, 2, 3...) until you feel good about doing the *process* (which is the *end-point* of the process).

The ultimate goal is to genuinely increase one's *Willingness-to-Reach* in whatever area is being treated, since ultimately a *"god-like"* being would be *willing* to *know, do, communicate* or *experience* anything, whether or not they actually choose to. There is another aspect to these *processes* that increases *willingness* to "grant" or "permit" others their own *"Beingness"* — to also allow others the freedom to *Be.*

Willingness To Find Out

1. *"What would you be willing to find out about yourself?"*
2. *"What would you be willing to find out about someone else?"*
3. *"What would you be willing for someone else to find out?"*

In this *process*, the phrase *"find out"* could be substituted with *"know."* And *"would you be"* is a basic, less intrusive, wording that is often used with beginning *Seekers*; but a more direct PCL approach is *"are you."* We will apply the direct approach here:

Willingness To Have

1. *"What are you willing to have?"*
2. *"What are you willing for someone else to have?"*
3. *"What are you willing for others to have?"*

In this instance, *"someone else"* means a specific person (*terminal*); whereas *"others"* is meant to include everyone in a particular group, for example: all other *"Humans."* Let's do some more of this *processing*.

Willingness To Do

1. *"What are you willing to do?"*
2. *"What are you willing for someone else to do?"*
3. *"What are you willing for others to do?"*

Willingness To Be

1. *"What are you willing to be?"*
2. *"What are you willing for someone else to be?"*
3. *"What are you willing for others to be?"*

When we speak of *willingness* and *accessibility*, we tend to also use the word "*tolerance.*" This means what is within an individual's *willingness* to *confront*. One of the areas that a *Seeker* may actually *process* for greater *tolerance* in general regards "change." The most basic *process* is to *alternate* the following PCL repeatedly.

A. *"What would you be willing to have change?"*
B. *"What would you be willing to have remain the same?"*

An *objective* example of this same *process* is:

"Look around the room; Spot some things you would be willing to have change?"
"Spot some things you would be willing to remain the same?"

One of the reasons that so much of our existence remains in the realm of "not-known" is because of our avoidance of actually *confronting* the contents of "what lies beneath." In many cases, there is a deeply laden *fear* that inhibits our *Willingness-to-Know*. Or a person stops "*looking*" and starts "*thinking*" and worrying from a point of confusion instead.

Knowingness is preferred to *thinking*. There's nothing inherently wrong with *thinking*, except that it usually originates from a *fragmented* state and is used to substitute actual *Knowingness*. The worst fears generally concern what is "*not-known*" (or "unknown"), and not what an individual actually understands or *knows*. So, let's just get some of that out in the open with this next *process*, before we continue.

"Think of, or imagine, a horrible 'truth' that you might find out."
"What would be the consequence of that?"

SYSTEMOLOGY & COMMUNICATION

Communication is a central subject to *Systemology*, because we consider *all interactions* between "systems" to be a "communication." In fact, "*Systematic Processing*" is entirely based on our understanding of communication from within the philosophy of *Systemology*. And in many ways, we are really treating various aspects of communication consistently all along the *Pathway*.

In *Systemology*, "communication" is *systematically* handled as a *flow*. This allows us to treat all types of communication; not simply the "speech" and "gestures" we quickly associate with it, in terms of the *Human* experience. *Flows* occur on a "*channel*" between two *terminals*—usually *you* and something else.

A *Seeker* may notice similarities between our *Systemology of Communication* and the way in which "*water motion*" or "*electricity*" is understood in other applications. Either of these could be used to demonstrate our principles. We will focus on "water" for the moment, rather than assume an understanding of *electricity*.

Running water is a type of *communication*. Although we treat it all inclusively as a "body" of water, it is actually composed of individual droplets, each of which might be thought of as a single "unit" of water. In a stream, the activity of *flow-motion* represents the communication. It allows a single "unit" to cross a *distance*, from a source-point to a destination-point within a certain period of *time*. Therefore, *motion* and *time* are connected.

Fragmentation is that which "blocks" *free-flow* on a *chann-*

el. It creates a "dam" for an otherwise fluid current. And as we know, concerning water blockages and dams, this has a tendency to build up "pressure." In our *processing*, this "pressure" is equivalent to the *"charge"* or *"turbulence"* that is encountered for a given area.

Inhibited communication, and control of these *flows* by outside (*other-determined*) sources, is what leads to our greatest upsets in life; it leads to violent protests, compulsions, reactivity, automation, and other societal misfortune.

Fortunately, control over these *"communication barriers"* ultimately remains our own. For, regardless of the reasons, it is ourselves (as an *Alpha-Spirit*) that decides to go "out-of-communication" with a *terminal*, or to relinquish *knowing* control over the *flow* on a particular *channel*.

With enough *actualized* or focused *attention*, you can systematically push through any personal *communication barrier* without even having to address all the reasons for its being there. In the case of "basic" *Human* communication, most barriers are crossed simply by *quantity* and *volume*.

For example: if you were to talk enough about a particular area, you would eventually find yourself uninhibited about communicating that subject. The reverse of this, or how we become inhibited, is when an "outside" (*other-determined*) source repeatedly demands (or even enforces with actions) that we *stop* that *flow* of communication each time we *start* it.

Systematic Processing resolves this by encouraging a *flow* until the barriers are cleared away. This is one of the benefits to *Traditional Piloting* for some *processes*; because another individual is there to keep those cycles of communication *flowing* along a *channel*, without the *Seeker* feeling the need to "*hold back.*"

Outside of our philosophy, a more familiar "*New Thought*" technique involves a practice of writing letters to individuals that we have difficulties communicating with—or about certain subjects. We don't actually send these letters, but it gets us to externalize a flow (out on paper) that is otherwise being held in. There is no pressure to actually engage in communication with the other person until we feel comfortable doing so.

If we were to extend this practice *systematically*, we would also include writing letters from the perspective (or *point-of-view*) of the *other* person, as if they are writing *to* us. This allows us to handle both the "*out-flow*" and the "in-*flow*" on a *channel*, between us and a *terminal*.

In *Systemology*, we also refer to these various *flow*-types as the "*circuits*" of a *channel*. These circuits are usually numbered: 1, 2 and 3. They correspond with the numbers given to the three PCL in many *processes*. They concern:

1, *out-flow*, what we project or send;

2, *in-flow*, what we receive; and

3, *cross-flow*, what we perceive or observe of others.

Communication is experienced on these three *circuits* of a *channel*; and on these same *circuits* we store our *fragmented data*. Let us see this directly in an example of "*communication processing.*"

1. "*What would you be willing to say to someone?*"
2. "*What would you be willing to have someone say to you?*"

3. *"What would you be willing to have someone say to others?"*

The PCL are *run* in rotation. The procedural instruction is to *"spot"* specific things that you are willing to communicate about. It is possible that there are many specific areas that require additional *processing* later in order to handle completely, so be sure not to invalidate the progress and gains that you actually do make along the way by feeling like you are still "avoiding" certain things.

This *process* is *run* until you feel an increased freedom in ability to communicate. The ultimate *end-point* on this would be total uninhibited communication about anything—regardless of what you actually choose to, or not to, communicate about.

An advanced upper-level application of this same *process* is included for consideration.

1. *"What would you be willing to 'read' in someone's mind?"*
2. *"What would you be willing to have someone 'read' in your mind?"*
3. *"What would you be willing to have someone 'read' in another's mind?"*

COMMUNICATION PROCESSES

The subject of *communication* is handled in various areas throughout the entire *Pathway*. Elsewhere, in more advanced material, we also treat movement of a *"particle"* as communication. For now, let us focus on what is most familiar for the *Human Condition*; mainly, observable communications that originate from a *lifeform*.

What is considered *magic* or *mysticism* is simply a handling of *communication* originating from an *Alpha* "spiritual" existence. This includes our own *"Alpha Thought"* or *"postulates"* as a *Spiritual Being* (separate and superior to a constructed *"Mind-System."* A *postulate* is a "decision for things "to be" or "not be." It does not originate from a "brain" or anywhere within *this* Physical Universe; it *impinges* on, or *perturbs* activity in, this Universe via a *communication* of *intention.*

Communication is a broadcast, projection or *out-flow* of something from one point to another, across some distance. In *Human communication*, the "words" and method of delivery are secondary factors to the actual *intention* itself. Before any words are chosen, or any visible activity occurs, an *intention* is made. There is also an intended *receipt-point* or "destination" for the *communication* to "arrive" at.

For example: when these *Professional Course* lessons are developed, there is an intended "message" and an intended "audience" for it. The choice of words and arrangement into lessons then follows thereafter. A *true communication* cycle only occurs when its "meaning" is *duplicated* at the receipt-point exactly as intended. *Professional Pilots* must be expertly trained and skilled in this area to deliver *processing* to others.

Where *communication* concerns the individual or *Seeker*, we are most concerned with *intention*—the increase of strength and clarity of *intention*. With enough *intention* behind the meaning, you might even say the wrong words and others will still be able to *duplicate* the understanding implied. There are all various kinds of phenomenon in the area of *communication* that we will practice here.

"Choose an object."

"Say 'Hello' to it repeatedly."

"Notice the point in space you are projecting each 'Hello'."

"Directly intend them to various specific points surrounding (or next to) the object."

"Now intently focus them right into the center of the object."

This is practiced with different objects until a *Seeker* feels they have a handle on projecting *intention* into specific points. Once this is practiced with a deliberate concentration of focus, a *Seeker* then performs the action more rapidly with various objects throughout the room, and *intending* to land the "*Hello*" in the direct center of each without having to strain (or lingering for more than a moment on one point).

"Invent a nonsense word and intend for it to mean 'Hello'."

Practice the previous exercises, but speak the "nonsense word" as you intend your *communication*. Then practice this with other random words that you intend to mean "*Hello*." The *end-point* on this is a greater sense that *meaning* and *intention* is separate from the words and sounds *communicated* from the "*Body*."

Practice projecting *intention* with force as you shout "*Hello!*" at the objects. Alternate this with "whispering" it; but the emphasis here should be on sensing the same strong *intention* regardless of volume.

Finally, practice intending your "*Hello*" silently. This doesn't mean just sitting there and "thinking" the word. Get the same sense of *intention* as when you were using words and sound to *communicate* it. Alternate this with speaking the word, until you can maintain the strength of the *intention* when silent.

"One-way" *flows* of communication can sometimes feel depleting if *run* too long in the same direction. You may have noticed that during a publicity event or workshop that the "Q-and-A's" or more personal "book-signing" segments take place *after* an individual lectures or reads. This allows a natural *replenishing* of *attention units* that have otherwise been directed or projected *outward* for a long period of time.

You can actually balance this out in the above *processing* exercises by *imagining* that the objects are saying "*Hello*" to you, placing you at the *receipt-point*. The emphasis here should be on also spotting the object as a *source-point* of the *communication*. [At no time do we expect the object to audibly say "*Hello*."]

ACKNOWLEDGMENT PROCESSES

In two-way *communication*, there is another component to a true cycle: *acknowledgment*. The message crosses a distance from a *source-point* to a *receipt-point*, and the "receiver" *acknowledges* that the message has been received. This completes a full cycle-of-action. Another cycle may then begin.

Compulsive attempts to *communicate* result from lack of *acknowledgment*. An individual continues to *outflow* until they can sense that their *intention* has been received. You may have observed this in everyday life, where an individual continues to basically say the same thing until the receiver finally says, "*okay, I get it.*"

In *Traditional Piloting*, acknowledgment is essential for completing a cycle or PCL. A *Pilot* directs the PCL; the

Seeker receives it and performs the action; the *Pilot* completes the cycle with an *acknowledgment*—usually "okay," "thank you," "all right," &tc. This is a critical part of *systematic processing* when it is "Co-Piloted." In *Solo-Piloting*, a *Seeker* still acknowledges to themselves (e.g. *"okay"*) when an action (or PCL) is completed.

An acknowledgment is also a communication—and therefore carries its own *intention*. In the everyday life example above, a person might intend their acknowledgment to mean either, *"okay, I see what you're saying"* or *"okay, I heard you a hundred times already, just shut up."*

Using the previous *"communication processes"* as a model of practice, let us do some exercises that concern the area of acknowledgment.

"Imagine objects in the room saying 'Hello' to you."
"Acknowledge each 'Hello' by saying 'Thank You' out loud."

As before, a *Seeker* can also practice this by intending a "silent" acknowledgment, once they have a sense for it with words and sound. And, as before, a sense of the actual *intention* is the emphasis of the *process*.

DUPLICATION AND REPRODUCTION

There are two main aspects of *duplication* that directly affect a *Seeker*—in *processing* or otherwise: the ability to duplicate an action (the same thing repeatedly); and the ability to copy the meaning of what is being communicated, or to even put an advanced spin on it, to duplicate someone else's *"point-of-view"* ("POV").

Ability to properly handle duplication is critical to the

"spiritual well-being" of the *Alpha-Spirit*. Having experienced a very long existence, an individual that has suffered from many undesirable incidents will likely go "out-of-communication" (or "out-of-reach") with such areas, finding it unacceptable that these things should repeat. This develops into automatic-reactivity that make us reluctant to repeat anything.

There is also the factor of *imprints* on the *Backtrack* remaining from lifetimes spent in slavery—often forced to do repetitive tasks under duress. There is a lot of *turbulence* in this area for most *Humans*, and it has caused an increase of unhappiness and illness when triggered or restimulated in modern society. Of course, if *"duplication"* is *processed*, a *Seeker* can experience a relief from the discomfort associated with it.

As has been the general method in these early lessons, we'll start with the *"Willingness"* to *duplicate*. This is a light *subjective process*.

1. *"What would you be willing to have happen again?"*
2. *"What would someone else be willing to have happen again?"*
3. *"What would others be willing to have happen again?"*

In this instance, it may be apparent that our systematic approach of revolving circuits is also meant to keep a *Seeker* from *running* a single *flow*-type for too long. Repetitive-style *processing* is sometimes *run* in *Co-Piloted* sessions, because ultimately we are mostly concerned with the first PCL. But for a *process* like this, a *Solo-Pilot* will assuredly not get the most significant results by continuously *running* that one *flow* alone.

"BELL, BOOK & CANDLE"

The *"2020 Professional Piloting Course"*—now collected in the *"Metahuman Destinations"* volumes—occurred shortly after release of the first two advanced publications: *"The Tablets of Destiny Revelation"* and *"Crystal Clear: Handbook for Seekers."* During this time, we spent a lot of time experimenting with methods of increasing a *Seeker's "presence in-session."* The subject of *"duplication"* sprung up continuously.

In the original version used at the *Systemology Society*: a bell, a book, and a candle, are all placed on the table in front of the *Seeker*. They select two of the items and the third is put away. This validates a *Seeker's* power of choice at the start of the *process*. This may be performed with *any* two *dissimilar* objects.

A version of this now appears in our modern practice (script) of a *Formal Session*, in the *"Opening Procedures"* listed as "Control of Body and Mind In-Session." In those instructions: the items are placed within reach; or alternatively, at two points in the room (preferably on tables), in which a *command-line* for "walking between" would be inserted in the *process*. [Objects are listed as *"Item-1"* and *"Item-2."*]

"Pick up Item-1."
"Notice its weight."
"Notice its color."
"Notice its texture."
"Put it down."
"Pick up Item-2."

"Notice its weight."
"Notice its color."
"Notice its texture."
"Put it down."

This is performed repeatedly over and over again; but it is not really as simple as it seems. Each cycle must be performed just as if it is the "first time" and *not* simply as an "automated repeat" action. One of our goals with this *process* is to *"run out"*—or *"process out"*—the reactive tendency of putting repetitive action "on automatic." It also treats the tendency of *re-creating* the *past* as the *present*.

To be extremely effective and provide stable results, it is not uncommon at first to *run* this *process* in excess of 20-30 minutes, and then for as long as an hour or two. This is not how it is treated as an *Opening Procedure* in a typical *Formal Session*; but, it may be when it is first introduced to a *Seeker* by a *Professional*. It is also not uncommon to experience the entire *"Beta-Awareness Scale"* of *emotional* and *mental* states while *running* this.

As a *Self-determined Alpha-Spirit*, there is nothing inherently wrong with setting a "system" or creating a "mechanism" to do things "on automatic" *knowingly* by choice. Unfortunately, there is a lot of this built into the *Human Condition* that is experienced *unknowingly*. Therein lies the *fragmenting* factor.

It is certainly within the capabilities of a *"god-like"* being to perform the same action repeatedly without giving in to any "hypnotic effect." Properly *running* "*Bell, Book & Candle"* allows a *Seeker* the practice of breaking "hypnotic effects" of repetition—but only when seeing each performance of the cycle as a "new action," intended in its own unit of time, and not the cumulative copy of the past.

There is an advanced application of this *process* that may be applied on additional passes through this material (if it is found to be above a *Seeker's* present skill level). A *Seeker* should be well practiced with the standard ("physical") version of this as given above—and *run* it for a few cycles in the same session before applying the advanced ("mental"-"eyes closed") version.

This practice works best if you are able to *imagine* or visualize a *"space,"* rather than simply *creating* the two objects in your mind. For example, you can image the corners of a cube or a room and then add the walls, floor and ceiling. Make this large enough that it extends above, below and behind the *viewpoint* (or "POV") that you are perceiving this imagery from. [There is *no* reason to imagine yourself as a *body* in that room.]

"Create (or 'imagine') two tables in the room."
"Create 'Item-1' on one of them; and 'Item-2' on the other."
"Intend for 'Item-1' to float up above the table."
"Notice its weight; Notice its color; Notice its texture."
"Intend for it to float back down."
"Intend for 'Item-2' to float up above the table."
"Notice its weight; Notice its color; Notice its texture."
"Intend for it to float back down."

Practice the steps in alternation, as with the standard ("physical") version.

Working through the first, second, and third lessons of the *Professional Course,* marks completion of "*Systemology Level-0.*" It demonstrates all of the skills necessary for a *Seeker* (or *Pilot*) to conduct a *Formal Session* and perform *systematic processing* for additional "levels" that remains on the *Pathway-to-Ascension.*

LESSON FOUR: HANDLING HUMANITY

HANDLING THE HUMAN CONDITION

In this lesson we will begin using the skills we previously learned for establishing a *Formal Session*—or rather, our *"presence in-session,"* which is what makes *systematic processing* possible.

Here we will start to apply *processing* to specific areas that are necessary for a state of *Beta-Defragmentation*. This means handling the *Human Condition* and *confronting* our experiences in this lifetime.

For the *processing* demonstrated in earlier lessons, we mainly encouraged simply "pushing through" any *resurfacing* or *restimulated fragmentation*. It is, however, at this level of the *Professional Course* that we begin to learn how to handle *fragmentation* directly—to start actually scraping away the layers of *imprinting* and the *considerations* about *Life* and *Reality* that have been made as a result.

This lesson is based on teachings previously given in the *"2020 Professional Piloting Course"* and contained in the text: *"Metahuman Destinations (Volume II): The Universe and Mind-Body Connection."*

[Note: if you have already attained any ultimate *realizations* as *end-points* for any particular area (from previous passes through this course material), then your practical instruction is to *"spot"* the moment it happened; alternatively if you have completed *Beta-Defragmentation* altogether, this material may be applied to *Alpha-Defragmentation* by *imagining/creating*, or apply the *processing* directly to the *"Backtrack."*]

COMMUNICATION AND PROTEST

Early on the *Spiritual Timeline* (or *"Backtrack"*), an *Alpha-Spirit* goes *"out-of-communication" knowingly* and selectively. This is part of how personal *Identity* is established. The *Alpha-Spirit* imposes or creates a certain "distance" for their *communication*, and "barriers" to their *perception*, so as not to experience being an integral of all *"beings"* at once.

It is in this wise that we can consider the individual's own *Spiritual Timeline* much like a *"personal identity continuum"* of an *Alpha-Spirit*—a *"ZU-Line"* that extends back to before the origins of even our "keeping track" of *time*.

As the "barriers" are originally *knowingly "Self-*imposed"—or *created* on one's own *Self-determinism*—they are usually able to be side-stepped early on the *"Backtrack"* easily with *intention*. But they are "barriers" nonetheless, and as a result, the *Alpha-Spirit* can still be "surprised" or suddenly encounter something that they weren't *aware* of, or prepared for.

Before an *Alpha-Spirit* begins to *"identify"* with *lower* material considerations for their own *Beingness* (what they truly consider *Self to Be*), they are essentially unable to be harmed—there is no "substance" for which to impact. Yet, as an early part of the formation of a basic spiritual *"identity,"* we still find the phenomenon of *"personal preference."* This might be based on *"aesthetics"* (our perception of *beauty* and *ugliness*), but it becomes an established pattern of *acceptance* and *rejection*—and increases the likelihood for blocked or misunderstood *communication*.

When undesired *communications* and *creations* are being forcefully presented to the *Alpha-Spirit*, or when their own *communications* and *creations* are rejected by others, the individual may decide to "protest" their experience of this enforcement or rejection. This is an activity modern society is quite familiar with, so we will avoid using examples that are *too* specific.

However, when an individual attempts to *communicate* a *protest* and finds they are "blocked" on those *channels*, or toward a particular "audience" (*terminal*), they will increase the volume, or *create* something that is much more "physical" in nature and therefore more difficult to ignore. Something is *created*, but it is still likely to be *rejected*, and so the individual goes on continuing to *create* it "compulsively."

Often times, a "*protest fragmentation*" may be found at the heart of a "*compulsion*"—or *compulsive creation*. This is why *processing* only toward one's own *acceptance* of its existence is not enough to overcome it. The main issues must eventually be handled concerning all *flows* or *circuits* on that channel: *rejection* or *lack of acceptance* in both directions—and even the observation of others *rejecting* someone else can affect our considerations.

Communication barriers are the first factor of *fragmentation* that an *Alpha-Spirit* experiences on the *Backtrack*. Of course, because they are *Self-determined*, they are not themselves the area of *fragmentation* we target as we begin our "*defragmentation processing*." It is "*protests*" that are the first actual source of *fragmentation* that actually lowers actual ability and *Awareness* of an *Alpha-Spirit*; in this case because of the *compulsive* activity.

The instructions for basic "*protest defragmentation*" is:

"spot" (*recognize*) a specific *protest*; identify what you are *creating* or *doing* to communicate that *protest*; and identify who should have received or acknowledged that communication.

A *Seeker's* "reach" on this direct method of *processing* may be limited during their first pass through the *Professional Course* material. Many of our *compulsive creations* we carry with us as *Spiritual Beings* are protesting things and aspects of existence that are not only long-forgotten, but far and beyond what is found in *this present* manifestation of a Physical Universe ("*Beta-Existence*"). As a *Seeker* increases what they *realize*, or are *aware* of, even more becomes accessible.

PROTEST DEFRAGMENTATION

As a standard *process*, the above instructions may involve communication with a *Co-Pilot*; or a *Solo-Pilot* may wish to record their answers in a "*Flight-Log.*" It is best to *run* the same area of *protest* repeatedly. Focusing on *spotting* it and describing its specifics with each *run*. This allows the *process* to naturally shift to an *earlier* "*protest*" in memory that is in the same area or along the same *channel*. This enables you to more fully *defragment* that entire "string" or "chain."

A. "*What are you currently protesting? Describe it.*"
B. "*What have you done to communicate that?*"
C. "*Who should acknowledge that communication?*"
D. "*Imagine them acknowledging your communication.*"

This same basic *processing formula* (for "Circuit-1") can also be applied to handling "*protests*" on other *flows* or *circuits*. It may be preferable to rotate these other *processes* in between *processing* your own *protests*, to keep from *running* only one *flow* excessively. The following steps apply to "Circuit-2."

A. *"What about you is someone protesting?"*

B. *"What have they done to communicate that?"*

C. *"How could that be acknowledged?"*

D. *"Imagine them receiving your acknowledgment."*

And for "Circuit-3."

A. *"What are others protesting?"*

B. *"What have they done to communicate that?"*

C. *"Who should acknowledge that communication?"*

D. *"Imagine them receiving the acknowledgment."*

As *systematic processing* becomes more intricate and specific in various areas, a *processing formula*—or basic *processing command-line* ("PCL")—is given in the text that is intended to apply to a specific *"terminal"* (a person, place, thing; something with "mass"). As a *Seeker* progresses on the *Pathway*, certain areas are found to be more turbulent than others, and are therefore targeted directly.

For example: *"What have you protested about ---?"* is directly applied to any specific area (or *terminal*) that is considered a source of *turbulence* or *fragmentation* for the *Seeker*. In *Traditional Piloting* there may be a list already prepared for a *Seeker* based on earlier sessions, or else something specific that requires additional handling. If the *answer* to this PCL is "nothing," than you simply move on to the next without pressing it further.

Without having a specialized list personalized for an individual *Seeker*, we will use some general *terminals* for our *processes*. These are:

"YOUR BODY"; "YOUR FAMILY"; "JOBS"; "SOCIETY"; "HUMANS"; "LIFE ON EARTH"; "THE PHYSICAL UNIVERSE"; "SPIRITS"; and "RELIGION."

Each represents its own *process*, and are used to complete the first PCL below.

The *processing formula* is:

A. *"What have you protested about ---?"*

B. *"What did you do or create to protest that?"*

C. *"Who should have acknowledged it?"*

D. *"Spot an earlier similar protest and repeat."*

A *Seeker* will generally *run* this until feeling increased relief in a certain area as an *end-point*. This type of *processing* is also helpful for those *Seekers* that at first do not find accessible answers to the more direct entry-level approach of *"What are you currently protesting?"*

When a *Seeker* is comfortable with the results of a particular *process*, or when an *end-point* is reached on what is presently accessible, deeper information may usually be "scouted" by reshaping the PCL or formula as a direction to "*imagine*" something. In this case, the wording could be changed to *"What might you protest..."* or *"What would be a communication..."* &tc. The goal being always to "shine" *Awareness* on new "layers." If, however, anything seems too out-of-reach for you right now, simply take it up on your additional passes through the *Professional Course*.

ACCEPTANCE AND REJECTION

A traditional way of scouting for (and handling) "protest fragmentation" attached to a particular *"terminal"* (or turbulent area), is PCL-alternation with a form of *"conceptual processing."* This generally assists a *Seeker* to free up their considerations or increase their tolerance.

A. *"What about --- might you protest?"*

B. *"What about --- could you accept?"*

Enforced inhibition—when we are prevented from *having, doing* or *being* something—often produces dramatizations of "protest." This can actually manifest in two ways. For one: there is the obvious "protest" that results from being denied something, and we still want it.

There is also another side: when this "something" is denied for too long, we may suddenly *consider* that it is "bad" and that we no longer want it. But there is still a need to connect with it on some channel, so the only solution is to "protest" *against* what we wanted but were denied, just to make sure *Self* is always right.

A. *"What have you been prevented from (having, doing, being)?"*

B. *"What protest might you have about that?"*

"Protesting" is a very specific type of *communication outflow*. Whatever that communication may be, it is quite pointedly directed at a target recipient (involving a specific *"terminal"*). Here we see one of many instances where material from our previous lesson on *"communication"* reoccurs on the *Pathway*.

The final *process* given for this area utilizes *Actualized Awareness* to "disintegrate" *fragmentation* directly. The theory behind its effectiveness is secondary to its application. However, let us consider that whatever we do not want around us, or in our space, is in some way being "protested against."

A. *"Get the concept of protesting the existence of ---."*

B. *"Now admire the existence of ---."*

C. *"Get the concept of you creating the existence of ---."*

This may be run repeatedly on something you are "protesting" the existence of, even if it is not concerning a dramatization of the "marching, shouting, picketing" type we are quickest to associate with the idea. We also commonly "protest" the *existence* of certain aspects regarding "school," "work," "family," and "social governance," that we experience as *reality*. But "protest" actually concerns any strong dislike or avoidance.

To be systematically effective, *protest processing* must be handled on the direct *existence* of something—and not "something about something." If you *process* a "dirt scuff" on your shoe: the protest is "the *existence* of the scuff," and not the fact that "the shoes have a scuff on them."

This systematic approach also helps us separate our *considerations* about what a thing *"Is,"* as opposed to focusing on *fragmented associations* directly. The *fragmentation* here would make us more inclined to eventually not like our *"shoes"*—or even develop some other kind of automatic-response about "shoes" in general.

The *"admiration"* step may require some "build up" (with each PCL-cycle) to really acquire a good sense of. At first, a *Seeker* might simply "acknowledge" the *existence* of the thing; but with each pass of the step, try and apply an even greater sense of "*admiring*" it than previously.

Again, we are mostly concerned with freeing up a *Seeker's considerations* and *perceptive* range—undoing compulsively created *imprints* and *automated* thought. What an individual *chooses* to like or dislike as a preference is just fine so long as they are totally *Self-determined* and *Self-Honest* in their *choosing*. A *fragmented* individual only operates on a false conception of having full and total *Self-directed* control.

CHANGE AND MOTION

As a *Seeker* expects to advance upon the *Pathway*, their *willingness* to "change" must be increased. When things are difficult, there is a tendency to "clamp down" and resist change in order to avoid things getting worse. This is dramatized automatically by the "*Body*" when hurt. Essentially, the individual is trying to hold things in place—and as this starts to happen more compulsively, it becomes more difficult to change for the better.

The *Alpha-Spirit* is, itself, a "*static*" point of *Awareness* that *can* develop a distaste for "motion" (and to an extent, the *control* of *motion*). To some degree, there is a tendency to *unknowingly* hold everything "*still*" as a protective defense-mechanism against danger or harmful effects. Likewise, a being tends to "*keep things from going away*" as a compulsive (*unknowingly repetitive*) remedy for the experience of *loss*.

Let's shift our focus now to some *objective processing* techniques for *"Change-and-No-Change."* Each of these cycles is done five times on the same object. When you've done all three on the same object, choose a different object and do them again, five times each.

A. *"Spot the object."*

   "Place your hands on it."

   "Hold it absolutely still."

   "Decide when to let go, and then take your hands off."

B. *"Spot the object."*

   "Place your hands on it."

   "Get a sense of keeping it from going away."

   "Decide when to let go, and then take your hands off."

C. *"Spot the object."*

   "Place your hands on it."

   "Decide to move it; Decide where to move it."

   "Move it to the exact spot you had decided on, and then take your hands off."

This same *systematic processing* formula may be applied to the *"Body."* For example: using your hands to grab your right leg and *"hold it absolutely still."* Then, doing the same with the other cycles: intending to *"keep it from going away,"* and then finally *"deciding to move it"* (using your hands to lift it up and down).

Note that to *"hold it still"* and *"keep it from going away"* only appear the same at a visible level. The key difference is that, in the second one, our *intention* also includes resisting any of its efforts to move away while "holding" it there. Essentially: *our intention* is to "stop" *its effort* to "change" (or move).

This can also be practiced on other parts of the body. In some ways, it starts to establish a habit of *controlling* the *"Body"* more deliberately or *"intentionally."* Specifically in this case, an individual is *knowingly* practicing an otherwise automatic (*unknowing*) reaction to "hold" an injured or painful part of the body.

As with many other *objective processes* in *Systemology*, there is also a more advanced "mental" version of this exercise. It is practiced much in the same way as the physical technique, except a *Seeker* reaches "mentally" rather than with the *"Body."* In the third step: rather than "moving" the object, the PCL is to *"make it more solid."* This is done by *intention* and *sensed conceptually*.

PROCESSING "CHANGE"

In *systematic processing*, "change" is a *channel*. It is not, itself, a *terminal*; it is a *channel* between *Self* and many potential people, places, objects, *&tc*. The *communications* on this *channel* involve the three basic "circuits" described in *"Lesson 3."* The following *process* demonstrates a slightly expanded version of these *circuits*.

1. *"What would you be willing to change in another person?"*
2a. *"What would you be willing to allow someone to change in you?"*
2b. *"What would you be willing to have another person change in themselves?"*
3. *"What would you be willing to have another person change in others?"*
0. *"What would you be willing to change in yourself?"*

In the above *process*, we also introduce *"Circuit-0"* for the first time in the *Professional Course*. It is not so much a communicative *flow* to others, but from *Self* to *Self*. In this case, *Self* is always the *"terminal."* In *Systemology*, this is sometimes referred to as a *"beingness postulate"* (or *"Alpha-Thought"*) when *Self directs* a decision that something *"Is"*—or about how something will either *"Be"* or *"Not-Be."*

In the end, all areas of *processing* are ultimately handling one's own *"postulates."*

In essence, it is *"Alpha-Thought"* that we are working up to reaching and mastering with the *Pathway*. If we were truly able to "change our mind" completely from within the *Human Condition*, we wouldn't remain in this state; so there are obviously some barriers of *fragmentation* that need to be cleared for this to be possible again.

To continue demonstrating how to *process* the area of "change," we will utilize the *"Analytical Recall"* technique introduced in *"Lesson 2."* Each circuit is treated in its own *process* containing two PCL. The PCL are alternated repeatedly until a *Seeker* cannot readily access more answers. Then go to the next *process* and do the same. After all four are completely *run*, cycle them again and see if any new answers are produced.

1a. *"Recall changing something."*

1b. *"Recall stopping something from changing."*

2a. *"Recall someone changing something."*

2b. *"Recall someone stopping something from changing."*

3a. *"Recall society changing."*

3b. *"Recall society resisting change."*

0a. *"Recall changing yourself."*

0b. *"Recall stopping yourself from changing."*

And now let's treat this more *"conceptually"* following the same basic instruction from the previous four *processes*. Notice we are using the words *"could"* and *"would"* to expand our range of free *consideration*.

1a. *"What could you change?"*

1b. *"What would you leave unchanged?"*

2a. *"What could change you?"*

2b. *"What would leave you unchanged?"*

3a. *"What could change others?"*

3b. *"What would leave others unchanged?"*

0a. *"What could you change about yourself?"*

0b. *"What would you leave unchanged about yourself?"*

For additional *objective processing* in this area:

"(Look around the room.) Spot something you would be willing (and able) to change; then change it."

"Spot something you find acceptable to remain the same; then leave it unchanged."

And finally:

A. *"What must be changed?"*

B. *"What must not be changed?"*

C. *"What is acceptable to leave uncontrolled?"*

D. *"What can you control comfortably?"*

As an entry-point to directly handling the *Human Condition*, we have emphasized the areas of "protest" and "change." Total *defragmentation* in these areas will likely take a second pass through the *Professional Course*, and possibly several cycles through the *processing* in this one lesson alone.

The ultimate *end-point* we are reaching for in this area would include the elimination of any compulsive tendencies in the areas of "protest" and "change." For example: a freedom from the *need* to change people, or prevent them from changing, in order to find them more acceptable. And, on the other side: an increased willingness to *allow* change in one's environment, or among others, without feeling a *need* to become involved.

HUMAN PROBLEMS

The type of *"problems"* handled with *Systematic Processing* are those things that tend to "hang up" in our lives—or else continuously exist without a perceivable solution. This is quite different from the kind of "logic problems" you might think of in relation to, for example, *"mathematics."*

Human Problems remain suspended in space and time as *fragmentation* because personal *attention-energy* remains compulsively fixed on them as a "problem." We are speaking of logical *"conflicts"*—or where two "things" (or *"considerations"*) remain fixedly in *opposition* to one another indefinitely.

For example: the *"problem"* of *how* to add additional rooms to your property is easily solved by logic. This would require a knowledge and means for construction, or hiring a contractor. This is not a *real* "problem." *Real problems* would require these two things to be *oppositional* —and they obviously are not.

But could this somehow become a *real problem?* Yes. If an individual *considers* that they both *"need an additional room"* and *"have no financial means to pay for it,"* then it could develop into a *"problem"* that suspends or fixes the individual's *attention-energy* compulsively.

These two things—*"needing rooms"* and *"no money for it"* are obviously in *opposition*. The conditions cannot exist simultaneously and ever provide any kind of "solution." When not properly handled, this kind of *problem* has a tendency to suspend *attention-energy* indefinitely, which is the nature of the *fragmentation*.

Ideally, an individual will *realize* that one side or other of the *problem* has to be figured out. It is not a balanced equation to be solved as itself. Yet, the longer it remains suspended as a *problem*, the greater of an *energetic-mass* it becomes as *fragmentation*. More and more *attention* is fed into it as purely a *problem*.

In this example, the only "solution" would be to treat either the *"need for more rooms"* or the *"lack of funds."* Both of these are *considerations* only. The fact that they collide during one's lifetime into a *mass* is simply unfortunate. Either an individual would have to find an *alternative* to the *"need for more rooms"* (such as better utilizing existing space), or they would find a way to *"make more money"* or build *"more economically."*

One of the reasons *Human Problems* unfold this way is because of how much *attention-energy* they demand once they are treated as a *mass*. They have a tendency to "pull down" an individual's *Actualized Awareness* in a way that keeps them from *considering* one "side" or the other, because they only "see" the *mass*.

When the *mass* becomes a turbulent source of *fragmentation*, it may have "grown" to a state that causes the individual to feel overwhelmed (*confused*) and unwilling to *confront* it.

For example: every time the individual starts to think about *"more room,"* the turbulence associated with *"money problems"* is triggered or *restimulated*, and hence they cannot think clearly about it. Then, whenever they start to try to *confront* the issue of *"money,"* the worries about *"space"* become a sudden distraction.

As you can see: this individual's *problems* will cyclically continue and persist in this wise unless there is some resolution or intervention from an outside source. Unless the *fragmentation* is solved, however, even good fortune and charity from others will not keep the individual from falling prey to this pattern again. Their thoughts and behavior will *unknowingly* still find there way into treating this *problem* as *reality*.

Our observation of this in others also inhibits our natural desire to *"help"* others. We've seen many times that our intervention to "solve" someone's *problems* directly will not always work out. They end up in the same mess again, or it somehow seems to "backfire" on *us*. This can cause us to develop *fragmentation* in the area of *"help"* which is quite detrimental to advancement on the *Pathway*.

The main areas for *systematic processing* that we focus on in this lesson, concerning *Humanity* and *Human Problems*, are: PROTEST, CHANGE, PROBLEMS and HELP.

DEFRAGMENTING PROBLEMS

The basic *processing* of *problems* begins with the PCL: *"What is the problem?"* This causes the *mass* to *resurface* directly. Then, a *Seeker* can *run* multiple cycles of: *"spot the problem"* and *"spot something about the problem"* and then *"spot the problem"* again. This allows a *Seeker* to start to control their *attention* in seeing the *"mass"* and then seeing a *"point"* of the *mass* rather than the whole. This may change how one *perceives* the *mass* thereafter.

When we say *"see,"* what we really mean is *"confront"* — and more specifically, *confront "As-It-Is."* This is something a continuing *Seeker/student* from previous lessons will be familiar with. Not only do we *process* toward *confronting* what the *Seeker* is presently perceiving as a *problem*, but in doing so, it is likely that other related or similar underlying *problems* will also *resurface* to confront — and this is how *defragmentation* ensues.

The standard *processing* method of the above technique is:

"What is the problem?"
"What part of that problem could you confront?"

Once a *Seeker* is able to "spot" both *opposing* "sides" of the *problem*, the most effective application for these types of techniques would involve alternately *"spotting"* (or *"confronting"*) something on *each* "side" of the *problem* as the *process* is repeatedly *run*.

An *Alpha-Spirit* is an *"eternal being"* that likes to be interested in things. *Eternity* is a long time — certainly long enough for us to have our fondness of *"games"* and *"solving problems"* get turned against us. In the case of the *Human Condition*, any lingering compulsive interests in *creating universes* and *games*, to add richness and variety to *Existence*, is reduced to *creating problems* for ourselves. By this we are always ensured to have "something" to *do*. A *fragmented* being will always prefer a *"fragmented somethingness"* over *"Nothingness."*

In these next *processes*, we are not trying to "solve" a *problem*. A *Seeker* "spots" the *problem* and then follows the next PCL, which starts with *"imagine."* By *"imagine,"* we mean to create, invent, or visualize something. This should be an original *creation* and not an automatically (*reactively*) *recalled* event or mental image, *&tc*.

By doing this *knowingly*, the *fragmentation* that causes the *"compulsive creation"* of *problems* comes into view, or at the very least "loosens" or "softens" for later additional *processing*.

The following three *processes* are *run* individually. If after *running* the first multiple times, the *problem* either seems more solid or the turbulence has not lessened, go to the next, and so on. They are all essentially working to accomplish the same thing and can be repeated as many times as is necessary.

"Spot the problem."

"Imagine a problem of similar magnitude."

"Spot the problem."

"Imagine something that is worse than that problem."

"Spot the problem."

"Imagine a game that would be more interesting than that problem."

A *real problem* is only brought to a *resolution* by handling it or *confronting* it *"As-It-Is."* Otherwise, whatever *fragmented* "solution" is applied to it will simply bury the original *problem* deeper and also create a new one. For example: *"borrowing money"* for the *"additional room"* only adds to the chain of complications attached to the original *"not enough money"* side of the *problem*. The individual still doesn't have enough and still has to pay for it, but now, presumably with interest. It only *avoids* the original "face" of the unsolvable *problem*.

We can apply some *processing* to this area by treating the stores of information colllected (communicated) on the "circuits." A continuing *Seeker* will, by now, be familiar with how to *run* this type of PCL-series:

1. *"Spot the problem."*
   "What solutions have you had for that problem?"

2. *"What problem has someone had with you?"*
   "What solutions have they had for that problem?"

3. *"What problem has someone had with others?"*
   "What solutions have they had for that problem?"

The total handling of *"a problem"* in *processing* is not the same as an *end-point realization* on the total area of *"problems"* in general; but it is a goal. Again, this is not something we are pushing a *Seeker* to expect on the first-pass of this course. However, the *"ultimate process"* for this area is:

"Spot the problem."
"What part of that problem could you be responsible for?"

This is *run* until a *Seeker* no longer produces new answers (or until the *end-realization* for the *problem* or problems). Then *run*:

"*Spot the problem.*"
"*What part of that problem could you admit to causing?*"

The ultimate *end-realization* on a single *problem* and the entire area of *problems* is: an individual is responsible for creating their own perceived problems. *Systematic Processing* is not intended as a "therapy" to "*solve problems*" but instead, a means of solving the need to handle or consider things *as real problems*.

ON THE SUBJECT OF HELP

"*Help*" is high-level *communication*. To be "*helped*"—to be *willing* to give and receive *help*—requires being *in communication*. Of course, we know that *help* is frequently taken advantage of, or even used as a control mechanism to enforce a *reality* on another. But to be *Self-actualized*, no *fragmentation* can inhibit our *willingness* to *help* and be *helped*.

Help is a difficult area for many individuals due to long *imprint*-"chains" comprised of many unfortunate experiences. Even when *help* is genuine—with "no strings attached"—it sometimes fails. When this cannot be *confronted* directly, the "weight" of accumulated failures builds up *mass* as "*help fragmentation.*"

As a high-power *flow* of *communication*, "*help*" also has the unique ability for breaking down or surpassing what would otherwise be a "*communication barrier.*" For example: if one could find ways in which to *help* an enemy and for an enemy to *help* them, the conceptual "walls" forged with hatred and war could dissolve.

When *Solo-Processing*, it is better to emphasize the "positive" side of an area in *processing*—or at the very least, being sure to alternate *spotting* the "positive" side along with the "negatives." Doing so assists a *Solo-Pilot* to push through the *fragmented-masses* that may have developed along these channels without too easily being overwhelmed by *turbulence* or distraction.

HELP DEFRAGMENTATION

In first approaching *Help-Defragmentation*, it may be best for a *Seeker* (as *Solo-Pilot*) to direct their PCL toward general "*terminal*" areas, rather than specific examples or individuals. This expands the range of *considerations* directly within the *process* (or during the *session*). It also promotes *defragmentation* on the greater "chains" that extend farther on the "*Backtrack*" (or personal "*Spiritual Timeline*").

Systematic Processing is really meant to improve how a *Seeker* handles an area in general. The seemingly current or presently restimulated "*problems*" and "*upsets*" that are more specifically targeted in some *processes* is merely a factor of *running* those areas. If something is presently triggering activity in a certain area, that would obviously require handling before one can get total stable control over that entire area.

Much like some of the other general areas of *subjective processing* already explored in the *Professional Course* series, we will use PCL that employ the words "*could*" in order to free up our *considerations* further *in-session*. This means that there is no pressure, directive, or insistence, that a *Seeker* actually "act" on any of these *considerations*. The "*answers*" do not all necessarily even have to be logical or realistic. We are simply treating all aspects of the entire area *systematically* in our *processing*.

These "*help-processes*" are the final *defragmentation* techniques provided in this lesson. They are simple *repetitive processes* using alternating PCL. A *Seeker* repetitively *runs* the PCL, simply *spotting* (*locating, identifying, recognizing in Awareness, &tc.*) the various ways you *could help* or *would be willing to help, &tc*. When cycling though these *processes*, a *Seeker* is often pushing through "mental barriers" of *consideration* and other *postulates* (or "*Alpha-Thought*") generated from a state of *fragmentation*. "*Answers*" may not always be immediately obvious, but they tend to *surface* in "layers." This applies to more than just *Help-processing*.

A *Seeker* may sometimes reach a point in the *process* where they really have to reach to come up with something and still its a struggle or they can't "find" an "*answer*" in their data-banks; but then something new "occurs" to them, and they suddenly start rapidly *outflowing* a whole new group of "*answers.*" This type of "*flash*" or "*sudden realization*" is a large part of what we are after when using these *processes*.

When listing your "*answers*" in *Solo-processing*, it is quite acceptable to simply "*read/run*" the PCL *once*, then write down as many answers that come to mind; or if you only come up with one or two and feel your mind kind of "wandering" afterward, then you might "*read/run*" again to reorient yourself. When you feel you have completed one *process*, simply go to the next.

Willingness to Help

1. *"Who or what would you be willing to help?"*

2. *"Who or what would you be willing to have help you?"*

3. *"Who or what would you be willing to have others help?"*

General Help Process

1. *"How could you help someone else?"*

2a. *"How could someone else help you?"*

2b. *"How could someone else help themselves?"*

3. *"How could someone else help others?"*

0. *"How could you help yourself?"*

Past Help (*four separate processes*)

1. *"What help have you given to someone?"*

   "What help have you not given to someone?"

2. *"What help has someone given to you?"*

   "What help has someone not given to you?"

3. *"What help have others given to others?"*

   "What help have others not given to others?"

0. *"What help have you given yourself?"*

   "What help have you not given yourself?"

To demonstrate more specific *Help-processing* in this lesson, it is necessary that we again employ a *processing formula*. Here, a *Seeker* uses the basic structure for separate *processes*, each of which may target a specific *terminal*.

Suggested terminals (in chronological order) for use are: "BODY," "CHILD," "PARENT," "LOVER," "TEACHER," "OFFICER," "PRIEST," "POLITICIAN," "ANIMAL," "TREE," "SPIRIT," and "GOD."

The *processing formula* is:

A. *"How could you help a ---?"*
B. *"How could a --- help you?"*
C. *"How could a --- help another?"*
D. *"How could another help a ---?"*
E. *"How could a --- help themselves?"*

What generally occurs when *processing* an area intensely —such as demonstrated with the above *Help-processes*—is that the individual's own personal *"definition"* for (or *consideration* of) a specific area—such as *Help*—changes many times. It is from the viewpoint or point-of-view (POV) of that new *"definition"* that the next layer of *"answers"* originates from. This is how a *Seeker* *"systematically"* frees their true power of choice.

Much of what is given as *Help-processing* really serves to assist in breaking down those "barriers" and *masses* that are *created* by the *Seeker*—even if *unknowingly*—which blocks their *Awareness* from truly contacting, experiencing, and therefore, *confronting*, this physical existence. It is only once these *"gates"* begin to be opened—once these *"walls"* we've *created* begin to break down—that we will *realize* we have only been sealing up our own entrapment this entire time.

- - - -

Working through this fourth lesson of the *Professional Course*, in combination with the previous three (and the *Basic Course*), marks completion of *"Systemology Level-1."* It demonstrates the first required step, an increase of *Actualized Awareness*, necessary to *actually* "improve"— which is to say, a *willingness* to "change" for the better— as the *Seeker* progresses further on the *Pathway-to-Ascension*.

LESSON FIVE: FREE YOUR SPIRIT

RELEASING THE SPIRIT

The previous lesson for this *Professional Course* series emphasized *"Handling Humanity"*—or else the *processing* of *Human Problems*. These areas included *"protest," "change,"* and even the subject of *"help."* It is important to handle these "surface areas" that seem to more visibly "press upon" or "interfere" in the daily experience of life, before setting our sights on higher vistas—such as we will approach in *this* lesson.

To begin this lesson, we will focus more directly on treating the *Seeker* (or *Self*) *as* an *Alpha-Spirit*. This is always the intention—because it is the actual *Self* or *I-AM-Awareness* as an *Alpha-Spirit* that we are treating with *Systematic Processing*; not a *"Body"* or even a *"Mind."*

It is the *Spirit* that we direct our *"processing command lines"* ("PCL") to when applying our philosophy as exercises or techniques. It is *Self* that processes the command, then either performs the action or directs that command to a *"Mind"* or *"Body"* if it is called for. Both the *"Mind"* and *"Body"* are *constructs*; *Self* is *Eternal*.

"Releasing the Spirit" is a continuous goal as a *Seeker* progresses further on the *Pathway-to-Ascension*, and it is composed of many parts. It is not necessarily a "practice" or "technique"—or even a single area—in itself. We are continuously interested in "freeing" the *Spirit* from the trappings of a material existence.

On the one hand, we have the *considerations* of *Beingness* that an individual experiences for themselves as an *Alpha-Spirit* (or in many cases, as restricted to the *Human*

Condition); on the other, we have the accumulated *fragmentation* that heavily "weighs" on the *Spirit*, and of which they are *compulsively creating* as "chains" that bind their *considerations* to lower-levels of material *Beingness* (*e.g.* the *Human Condition*).

It is a *cycle*. And in this lesson—as we start "*Systemology Level-2*"—we will explore and *process* each side of this re-occurring *cycle* directly.

SPIRITUAL BEINGNESS

In our basic state—back behind all the circuitry of "*Mind-Systems*" and "*Bodies*"—we are a single unit of *Spiritual Awareness* (or "*ZU*"). In the past, philosophers that have come close to a true understanding have associated this true "*Spiritual Self*" as "pure thought."

To say that we are "*thought*" and that everything is "*Mind*" is only a part-of-the-way-there kind of truth. It at least demonstrates an understanding that *Self* is not a "*Body*." For some, this itself is milestones ahead of identifying exclusively with a "*Body*"; or certain *body parts* used to "*think*" with (as the expression goes).

The *Alpha-Spirit* is not composed of physical matter or energy; nor is it dependent on it for its own existence. In actuality, we are an *Awareness* with the ability to generate and observe *thought*. We also have the ability to *create energy* without requiring an "outside" *source*. A full *Knowingness* of all this is what we seek to reclaim ultimately with our *Ascension*.

There are spiritual philosophies and metaphysical traditions teaching about various *"astral"* and *"subtle" bodies* that also enshroud the *Alpha-Spirit*. These do exist—and we presume that they are metaphysical constructs used by the *Alpha-Spirit* in former *Universes*, or less "physically solid" (less condensed) versions of *Beta Existence*. However, none of these are the true "pure" *Spirit* either.

In our native state, we are not located, or even locatable, in "space-time"—because our existence *precedes* the *creation* of *Universes* to be located in. The idea of *Self* being "located" in a specific spot is really a matter of *reality-agreements* for the practical purposes of, for example, participating in a "game" far more than a matter of "actual fact."

A *"Free-Spirit"* can locate its *Awareness* (as a "point-of-view") anywhere it chooses simply by *intention*. This means, when not "entrapped" by *fragmented considerations*, one should be able to be *in* the *"body"* or *out* of it, at will. One should also be able to freely *pervade* their own *"Mind"*-construct, and be in total control of it.

The traditional *"astral work"* that is found in contemporary "New Age" material differs greatly from the type of *"spirit vision"*—or *"ZU-Vision"*—that is sought with the practice of *Systemology*. Most *"astral"* work is still very much entangled in the *Mind*, even if *Awareness* is separated from a *body*. Our practices are directed at points of *Awareness* superior to all the various energy fields and subtle bodies.

"ZU-Vision" is treated more directly at higher levels of *Systemology* work—but there are many reasons why we introduce the concept earlier on the *Pathway*. Most importantly, it is a "phenomenon" that *may* be encountered early on the *Pathway*—especially during the practice of

"*objective processing*" (as given in earlier lessons), particularly when one is practicing the "advanced mental versions" of those techniques.

The pure *Spiritual Awareness* or *Alpha-Spirit* is the actual YOU—your *Self*—and it is quite capable of directly *creating*, *operating* and *perceiving* independent and exterior to *any* "*Body*." However, as beings entrapped by our *considerations* for *Beingness* within *this* "*Physical Universe*," we are primarily dependent on an "*organic-body*" (or "*genetic-vehicle*") in order to relay to us the sensory information of this existence.

Unfortunately, without achieving a high state of *Knowingness* during one's lifetime—from which *Ascension* may be reached—as an *actualized* state of *Awareness*, the metaphorical "gravity" (or "pull") of the *material world* and accumulated *fragmentation* (kept in all these "subtle" *bodies*), "weighs" heavily on *Self*; and it will continue to linger about looking for another similar "*body*." We do not automatically become *Free-Spirits* imminently at "death."

"ZU-VISION" AND PROCESSING

There are some *systematic processes* that prompt a *Seeker* to place their *Awareness* "exterior to" a *body*. By this, we do not simply mean "place their *attention*"—but to literally "*Be*" outside of the *body*. In actual practice, we do not mean "taking flight on some out-of-body journey"—but a stable ability to "stand outside" the *Body-Mind* systems and continue to control their operation as something altogether separate from *Self*.

This may happen earlier on the *Pathway* while *processing*, although its direct handling is reserved for upper-level *"Advanced Techniques"* (*A.T.*) of *Systemology*. However, we take this up now to provide a *Seeker* some sense of familiarity in case the phenomenon begins to occur; and there are some fun *processes* to *run* on this even if it has not happened.

A *Seeker* might experience the phenomenon very "suddenly" without intending to. This is a natural part of some of the *objective processing* when *run* for long periods of time. Although there is no danger in it, the "suddenness" and "unexpectedness" of the occurrence can affect later attempts to do this *knowingly*.

It usually is not the "getting out" part that causes *fragmentation* in this area, but the sudden "snapping-back-in" to a *body* that results from being startled by the phenomenon, or if the *body* is disturbed in its physical environment. This can create a *turbulent charge* on the entire subject, which of course makes later applications more difficult.

In an ideal situation, the *Alpha-Spirit* is *defragmented* and can easily move "in" or "out" without any sensation of "impact"; however, when the phenomenon occurs unintentionally, or an individual "gets out" carrying a lot of their *fragmented energetic-masses* with them, the sense of "impact" *can* be uncomfortable.

Barriers that hinder the *Awareness* of this native state and ability of the *Alpha-Spirit* are broken down little by little with *systematic processing*. This means that a *Seeker* is likely to experience the sudden phenomenon of "*ZU-Vision*" (perhaps for the first time, *knowingly*) during a *processing session*. Having some sense of this ahead of time will ease any worries and prepare a *Seeker* to handle it, if and when it does occur naturally.

In these early practices, we are not concerned with actually pulling your "normal" *point-of-view* (or "POV") of *Self*—and all of its "mental machinery" and "energy bodies" *&tc.*—out from their "usual" positions. And this is not necessary at this juncture of the *Pathway*, for the *Alpha-Spirit* (not being actually locatable itself) has an ability to establish more than one POV simultaneously, and in multiple locations.

A *viewpoint*—or *"point-of-view"*—is a "point" *from* which to "view," or else "operate" our *Awareness*. In basic terms, all you would need to do to *create* a *second* (or *alternative*) one is to decide on a *spot* (or *point*, if you prefer) and start operating as an *Awareness* from it. You may leave your previous ("normal") *Human* POV where it is for these early practices, and simply *add* an additional one.

The actual YOU—the *Self* or *Alpha-Spirit*—is always *present* (providing *presence*) wherever *attention* and *Awareness* is oriented or directed. So, *you* are never using a POV "*remote*" from *you*—but in this case, we mean a POV that is *remote* from the *body*. This is what makes common use of the term "*remote viewing*" misleading.

LOCATIONAL "POV" PROCESSING

Locational or *"POV" Processing* first appeared in the "*Imaginomicon*" volume of the *Systemology Core*. This practice is inspired by mystical training techniques found in *Franz Bardon's* work (see *Basic Course, Lesson-5*). Therein, *"transference of consciousness"* is described—where an *initiate* practices imagining their POV "going inside" solid masses (objects) that are separate from the *body*.

However, the original methods all seem to emphasize *flow* in *one*-direction only: the "going in" part. We can improve this practice for our *systematic processing* by using alternation: "going in" and "going out"—with repetition and fluidity.

Early experiments by research-members of the *Systemology Society* demonstrated that, initially, the best results come from practicing with "large" masses—ones that a *Seeker* is already familiar with, but which are not present in the immediate vicinity. Our standard instruction at the *Mardukite Academy* is to use "a mountain" (one which the individual is not already sitting on, if that is the case).

In *Traditional Piloting*, a *"Co-Pilot"* is not likely to have an objective reality on the *Seeker's* experience—or see whether or not the actions are being carried out. To remedy this: a *Seeker* may sometimes say *"okay"* after completing an instruction—or if a bit of time has passed in silence, it is customary for a *Pilot* to inquire, *"did you?"* This inquiry should not relay a tone of skepticism, but simply to prompt additional communication.

These practices found in *"Systemology Level-2"* do *not* demand a *Seeker* to have already achieved the much higher-level goal of completely separating from the "normal" *compulsively created POV* of *Beingness* "in a body." This *process* is practiced by *"imagining"* a *secondary viewpoint*. There is no reason to imagine some *"mental body"* (or any connected "cords" or "threads") in order to *create* or *visualize "mental imagery."*

A better understanding of a *secondary viewpoint* or *POV* is achieved by direct practice. The traditional *"Locational POV" processing command-lines* ("PCL") are:

A. *"Imagine being above (a mountain) looking down on it."*
B1. *"Imagine your viewpoint moving in to it."*
B2. *"Imagine your viewpoint moving out from it."*

In this formula, a *Seeker's attention* and *presence* are oriented in the first PCL; the last two PCL ("B1" and "B2") would be alternated repeatedly.

It is expected that most of what a *Seeker* first experiences with this *process* is purely *"imagination"* — meaning that it is *Self-created* in the absence of actual perceptions. Eventually, with practice, a *Seeker* will find that more of their *Awareness* is able to be "established" or "present" in the *secondary viewpoint*.

Recognition of "real perception" with this practice may be subtle at first, but still seem quite real. This is what we would mean by stably *establishing* a *secondary viewpoint* that is "remote" from the *body*. It is *secondary* and *remote* only to the POV that we apply to the *body* and experience with its eyes.

During phases of early progress on the *Pathway*, it is important to acknowledge any personal success or improvement in these areas by simply *ending* the *process*. To continue such practices further without a break may result in some anomaly that causes you to invalidate the gains that were made and feel like all of it was entirely imagined. Consider any "win" as an *end-point*. At the very least, return to it after a break.

Eventually, you would practice this beyond the point of

establishing a viewpoint in order to continue practicing "*Locational POV*" at a higher-level of application. For example: using a "New Age" suggestion from an "Eastern" technique called "*journeying to other planets*," we modified the above *process* to include practicing "*Locational POV*" with *any imagined* point in the *Universe*.

A. "*Be near (or above) ---.*"

B1. "*Be inside of --- (it).*"

B2. "*Be outside of --- (it).*"

C1. "*Be at the center of --- (it).*"

C2. "*Be outside of --- (it).*"

D1. "*Be on the surface of --- (it).*"

D2. "*Be above --- (it).*"

As an extended process: after a *secondary viewpoint* is established ("A"), each set (e.g. B1 and B2, *&tc.*) are alternated a few times in sequence—working from B to C to D; and then the whole B-C-D cycle is repeated again. Although the *running* of this *process* could be essentially "unlimited," find an appropriate *end-point*.

ADVANCED APPLICATIONS

An entire volume of material—"*Imaginomicon*"—is dedicated to the theory and practice of "*creativeness processing*." The work explored thus far in this lesson falls under that category. These applications have nearly unlimited potential variations. There are many suggestions we can review from that earlier material.

For example, with our original practice of setting up a *secondary viewpoint*: once a *Seeker* has certainty on their ability using a single *alternative POV*, the practice is expanded to include multiple *viewpoints*.

To begin, before considering *additional alternative POV*, a *Seeker* would initially practice by simply alternating between a created *secondary viewpoint* (with eyes closed) and the *POV* of the *body* when eyes are open.

This would mean "*anchoring*" your *alternative POV* above the "mountain" with an intention of "keeping it from going away." Once it is held steady in imagination, a *Seeker* should be able to resume that *viewpoint* (by intention) immediately upon closing their eyes.

Then alternate between viewpoints, spotting something in each: eyes open, *POV-1*; eyes closed, *POV-2*; and so on, until one feels satisfied to end the process.

As an additional gradient of practice, a *Seeker* can increase their *actualized perception* enough to simultaneously "*look*" through both *POV* (with eyes open).

It will be noticed, of course, that the "volume" or "amplitude" of the *perceptions* received from the *body-POV* are considerably "louder" than the *alternative-POV*. To improve on this, even with eyes open, all a *Seeker* has to do is increase the *attention* that is directed to the *alternative-POV* (to keep it from going away).

CREATION-OF-SPACE

The *Alpha-Spirit* has forgotten its own natural ability to *create* and handle "*space*." We have come to rely on the energy-matter of the *Physical Universe* and the sensory perceptions of a *genetic-vehicle* to have any sense of *"space."*

Although the concept of *imagination* and *mental imagery* is treated quite lightly in former instruction, the upper-level consideration is: to truly *create* energy, matter and various forms, there must first be *"space" created* for them to exist in. Although difficult to fathom for some readers at first, this is a concept that may actually be practiced in *processing*.

Many mystical practices treat philosophical constructs of *"space"* as "circles" and "spheres." For example: a "magician" *casts* a "circle" to mentally differentiate their own designation of "sacred space" from the surrounding universe. This is an example of dramatizing or mirroring *creation* of a *"Personal Universe."*

Using our methods, we developed a similar exercise that allows a *Seeker* to more *systematically* define the parameters of *created space* by using the philosophical construct of a "cube." A *Seeker* is likely already familiar with the idea of a "cube-like room" to designate a *"space"* as separate from elsewhere. This is far more effective in *processing* than mentally defining the three-dimensional points that compose a "sphere."

Our previous exercises is extended further for a demonstration of this idea. Rather than use the *facsimile-copy* of a "mountain" as we *re-created* it from something found within this *Universe*, this time we want to actually *imagine* the "mountain" being within the *"space"* of one's own *created "Personal Universe."* This is practiced by:

A. Creating dimensions (defining boundaries) of *"space"*; and then

B. Creating the energetic-masses or forms within that "*space*."

Rather than closing your eyes and essentially "*recalling*" an actual "mountain" from memory in order to duplicate a *facsimile-copy* of the scene, this time we want to *create* fixed dimensions of finite *space* within our *Personal Universe* for which to *imagine* "a mountain" of our own unique design.

Of course, "*Creation-of-Space*" may be practiced cumulatively over the course of multiple *sessions*. It is dependent on a *Seeker's* ability to *imagine (create)* and perceive a single "*point*" with definitive certainty.

This exercise is then extended to include other "*points*," a "*line*" between two points, a "*square*" composed of four points and four lines, and finally a complete "*cube.*" Eventually, a *Seeker* works up to being able to distinctly *perceive* the eight "*points*" to form a "*cube*" of "*space*" within a single *processing* "step" or PCL.

For our technique to be effective, when first starting out: it is far more important to distinctly and fully *create* and *perceive* a single "*point*" — and then even a "*line-segment*" between points, perhaps during a separate *session* — rather than rush progress and only vaguely have certainty on having *created* a stable "*cube.*"

Once the "cube" has been sufficiently *imagined*, a *Seeker* may then practice "*intentions,*" such as: "*hold it still,*" "*keep it from going away*" and "*make it more solid,*" to establish greater vividness of the *mental imagery*. [Refer to *Lesson-4* for details regarding use of these PCL in *processing*.]

If it is helpful, these "*intentions*" ("*hold it still,*" &tc.) may be applied (as PCL) to each progressive "step" (the *point*, the *line*, *&tc.*) along the way. Note that it has taken some Seekers a significant amount of practice to simply achieve a total *realization* of *creating* and "holding" even a single point "still" enough to perceive it "solidly."

The original *processing* steps are as follows:

"Imagine a point."

"Imagine a line stretching to a second point."

"Imagine lines stretching upwards from those two points to another two points."

"Imagine the upper points are connected to form a square."

"Imagine another set of four points connected together to form a second square."

"Imagine lines connecting the two squares to form a cube."

"Imagine that this cube is pure space."

Once a *Seeker* is skilled in this practice, *processes* (such as "the mountain") that involve *creating* or *imagining* (as opposed to *recalling*) are far more effective when handled within this personally *created space*. For example: rather than closing your eyes and suspending "a mountain" against the background scenery of your mind, you would first *imagine* a large *"cube-of-space"* and *then* the "mountain" within it.

THE "MUSTS" & "CAN'TS" OF LIFE

Part of the freedom that is recovered in *systematic processing*, is the ability to operate the *Human "game"* without obsessing over *"must haves"* and *"can't haves"* — or the flip-side of this, the *"must avoid"* and *"can't get rid of"* — considerations that seem to so strongly influence our thoughts and actions; or, at the very least, entangle much of our *attentions*.

There are times you may have noticed that when you had *really really* "wanted" something, it tended to remain out of reach; or when you have tried *really* hard to "avoid" something, it seemed to seek you out and practically land on your doorstep. This frustration is a part of the standard-issue *Human Condition*.

By "*must have*" we don't mean, for example, how a "body" *must have* "oxygen." We mean *intense "desire."* That being said: we aren't implying that you can't really like something and still obtain it, or have it. But, cravings and obsessions are born from *fragmentation*. The more *turbulent*, *fragmented*, or "desperate" the *attention* or *effort* given by someone, the more difficult it is to "manifest" exactly what they actually want.

Those things which we want (or don't want) are, indeed, "*things*," which is to say "*terminals.*" As such, our experience with them is based on *energy-flows* and *considerations*.

In the case of our usual (and often *fragmented*) participation with *Life*: that which we "reach" *too hard* for will create a "pressure-wave" type *flow* that will actually push the "thing" away; and when we try to "avoid" something *too hard*, we create a "suction-wave" type *flow* that will actually draw the "thing" toward us.

At an upper-level of understanding, attempts to *control* the *flow* using considerations of "*must have*" or "*can't have*" creates an energetic turbulence similar to what we encountered in *Lesson-4* concerning "*Human Problems.*" Of course, in that instance ("*problems*"), two basic things in opposition are colliding with each other; here we are specifically considering attracting things we desire and avoiding the undesirable.

There are times when the *clear route* seems "*counter-intuitive*"—but, then we must remember that in most cases our "*intuition*" is likely to also be "clouded" by *fragmentation*. And the real fact is: as we progress on the *Pathway*, our dependency on what some call "*intuition*" is gradually replaced by *true Knowingness*.

True *control* of a "system" often requires only a light touch. In the case of handling "*terminals*," we are again concerned with one's own level of acceptance. By this we mean *defragmenting* an area (or a *terminal*) to a point where a *Seeker* is *willing* to "have" or "not have" freely. This is the secret key to "*having*."

By being free of the *fragmentation* related to something, an individual is more likely to "enjoy" it without experiencing the interference of *compulsive obsessions*. In the same wise, *fragmentation* inhibits us from simply walking away from something we are disinterested in, without recoiling in revulsion and disgust.

DEFRAGMENTATION TECHNIQUES

Some of the best *systematic processes* for handling the "*must haves*" of *Life* utilize "*visualization*" or *creating* "*mental imagery.*" A continuing *Seeker* has had some practice with this already. While some may consider this to be "imaginative-play" only—we are still *systematically processing* our *considerations*. In this case, we use "*mental imagery*" directly to do it, rather than representative words to consider an area.

When we desire or crave a thing intensely, it has a tendency to develop an *automatic consideration* in the "Mind-System." This *consideration* is that the thing has near-infinite value and scarcity or rarity. Such *considerations* conflict with other *reality-agreements* we have about the "*Physical Universe*" when it comes time to encounter or manifest the condition of *having* whatever "it" is.

The systematic solution—although this will seem strange to some readers—is to visualize "*wasting*" (and then eventually "*giving away*") that which we *want* to *have* so deeply and keep so closely. At first, a *Seeker* might visualize the item being sucked into a vacuum machine or being thrown out into space. Then you can start to *imagine* actually giving it away to others.

This not only increases our fluid "*acceptance*" about the item; it also changes our underlying *perception* or *consideration* of the thing being "so super rare that we probably can't ever have it anyway." Only after this point is reached would an additional step be added of *visualizing* "*receiving*" it from others.

On the other side of this, we have also discussed the idea of obsessively "avoiding" certain undesirable things that seem to always show up in our lives. We have a *fragmented* view of "scarcity" in our lives. The same mechanisms are in play as before, but in reverse. In this case, you would start the previous technique with visualizations about *having more* of an item. The "*giving away*" and "*receiving*" parts remain the same.

These types of *processes* are not meant to be *run* for excessively long periods; but long enough to feel the "release point" of breaking through a certain "mental barrier" that has been restricting the free-*flow* of energy on the channel (as related to a specific "*terminal*," *&tc*). The *endpoint* is not so much of a *realization* as it is a certain "feeling" that some small weight has been "relieved" or has "fallen away."

This technique is not intended to actually "manifest" the condition of actually *having* something; only freeing up the *considerations* about *having* it, which is the required step (often missed) to getting what we want. To get a better sense of how this may be applied to various *terminals*, we'll take up an example.

"*Money*" is a good example to start; it is a general area of concern—and a common area of *turbulent fragmentation*. But, it is a good direct example—because, "*money*" is the equivalent of "*lifeforce energy*" that *flows* in a "human society." It is an integral "system" of "civilization"—and to operate at optimum efficiency, this *energy* must "circulate"; it must *flow*.

Using the above *process*, a *Seeker* would start by *imagining* ways to "*waste money*." It essentially "answers" a PCL for considering what physical actions one might take to "*waste money*," but by *visualizing* various scenes and possible events. *Imagery* should be *created*, not *recalled* from actual memory; and it can be completely ridiculous examples (*e.g.*, "tossing it into a fire"), so long as "*ways to waste money*" is answered.

Once a *Seeker* has worked with this, the additional steps of *processing* may be applied as *circuits*.

1. "*Imagine giving 'money' to someone.*"

2. *"Imagine someone giving 'money' to you."*

3. *"Imagine someone giving 'money' to others."*

In many ways, "forms" and "things" are the materialization of a particular "idea" or "concept." In the case of "*money,*" it is really a form of communication exchange that is used in exchange for various goods and services. This, again, makes it a perfect demonstrable example of the next *process*.

A. *"What could 'money' be a substitution for?"*

B. *"What could substitute 'money'?"*

Since one our goals is to freely accept and reject the same "thing" (as an *energy flow*), the following applies to more specific considerations:

A. *"What 'money' could you accept?"*

B. *"What 'money' could you reject?"*

Since we are dealing with a "thing" that we want (or don't want), we treat this type of *processing* differently than just the "concept" of the "thing" alone. If this were purely "*conceptual,*" we would run: "*What 'about money' could you...*" which is a slightly different, but related matter, introduced in previous lessons.

When the more significant turbulence has been quieted down for a particular area, only then is it appropriate to apply other types of "*affirmation*" or "*visualization*" techniques that might directly "attract" a particular energy or *flow* into your life. These are what are more commonly dispensed in typical "*Self-help*" and "*New Age*" material, but without actually handling the underlying *turbulence* or *fragmentation* itself.

As a result, many are turned off by any new "meta-psychological" approach, because the old *"think happy thoughts"* or *"wish it, will it, get it"* or *"help me, help you, help me, sell more pop-Self-help books"* didn't produce the stable results promised. A few people may have been the richer for it; mainly the authors. *Systemology* is not intended to be viewed in this same light. Our results speak for themselves with each individual *Seeker*.

To experiment with our philosophy further, using a *"New Thought"* exercise (in the direction of "fluidity" and "attraction"), try the following visualization exercise with your eyes closed.

Imagine "clouds" of "money" around your body. Then using *intention*, "push" those "clouds" into the body. Be careful not to "pull" them from the "inside" as this only reinforces the sensation of *Beingness* as a body. After doing this several times, *Imagine* these "clouds" and use *intention* to "throw them away" or else "explode" off in the distance. Then alternate back to *imagining* and *"pushing them in."* If either of these *"flows"* seems more difficult—or suddenly becomes more difficult—then concentrate on doing the "other" a few more times before alternating.

In the beginning of the exercise, it is easier to *imagine* handling "smaller" or "lower-grade" versions of the item (*"money"*) and then gradually improve the "value" represented (for example, "copper" into "silver" into "gold" *&tc*).

After you have worked through this material concerning *"money,"* consider applying the full cycle of *processing* given in this *"defragmentation"* section of the lesson to various things like: "FOOD," "SEX," and "JOBS" (or "WORK") for additional practice.

Eventually, a *Seeker* will want to *run* this on the actual (specific) stuff they *"really really want"* (and perhaps haven't been able to get, or blatantly *"can't have"*). The *"desires"* that run strong with an individual will be uniquely specific to them and cannot be covered fully here; but the same *procedure* given above is applied.

"AVOIDING" & "GETTING RID OF"

Having treated the area of *"wants," "must haves"* and *"can't haves"* above, the next step is to consider the other side of this: that which a *Seeker* feels they *"must avoid"* in *Life*, but can't seem to *"get rid of."*

Although we are treating all of these areas with words, at an upper-level, we are really handling the *energy-flows* of *attention*—and the *energetic-masses* that these form when *flowing* in one-direction too long. We can become so concentrated and fixed upon something that our *attention-energy* actually builds up a "pressure-like force" or "mass" that continues to press against something *oppositional* or *blocking*.

For example: when we were treating the area of *"must have,"* we began our *processing* by *knowingly* reversing the "stuck" (or *compulsively* "one-way") *flow* regarding the *terminal*, and *"wasting"* it, or *"throwing it away."* Once the *turbulent fragmentation* is handled, the *"acceptance-and-rejection"* type of *processing* simply provides greater stability (or certainty) for handling that *flow fluidly*.

In order to *systematically process* an *attention-flow* regarding the opposite—something that won't go away, or that a person is trying to be rid of (or avoid)—the first PCL of the previous *procedure* would be opposite. This means reversing the *flow* by *imagining* ways of *"having more"* rather than *"wasting."* The remainder of the *processing*—concerning *"giving-and-receiving"* and *"acceptance-and-rejection"* is identical.

For the previous demonstration, we used *"money"* as a common general example of something *desirous* to *have*. For this opposite demonstration, we will also use something general and common that most lifeforms dislike strongly and try to avoid: *pain*.

Usually this "reflexive" or "compulsive" use of our *attention* will cause us to attract more of what we are obsessively trying to avoid and/or to experience it more vividly when it does occur.

As a quick rundown of procedure, the first PCL (of the first *process*) is: *"Imagine ways to have more pain."* The remainder of the *process* consists of: *"Imagine ways to give 'pain' away"* and *"Imagine ways to receive pain."*

It is important, again, to *create* and not to *"recall"* actual events for this type of *processing*. Once a *Seeker* has *run* this, the *processing* may be applied directly as *circuits* as given here:

1. *"Imagine giving 'pain' to someone."*
2. *"Imagine someone giving 'pain' to you."*
3. *"Imagine someone giving 'pain' to others."*

And for the considerations:

A. *"What could 'pain' be a substitution for?"*
B. *"What could substitute 'pain'?"*

And finally:

A. *"What 'pain' could you accept?"*
B. *"What 'pain' could you reject?"*

If you were to apply the final *"visualization exercise"* from the original *procedure* above, than you would *imagine* "clouds" of "pain" around you—alternating the *"push in"* on the body and the *"throw away"* steps. As an extension of the *procedure* (for both sides), a *Seeker* can then *imagine* the representation of it and alternate *running* concepts of "connection" and "separation" (or disconnection).

A. *"Get the sense of being connected to it."*
B. *"Get the sense of being separate from it."*

This is *run* until a *Seeker* no longer feels any *compulsive creation* of a one-way "stuck" *flow*; which is to say, there is no longer a *flinch*, *craving* or *reactive-response* regarding that "channel" (to a particular *terminal*). Again, this regimen runs into areas that will apply uniquely and specifically for each individual, so the best we can provide in this *Professional Course* is a series of *processes* that have the widest possible *application*.

LESSON SIX: ESCAPING SPIRIT-TRAPS

BEING AT CAUSE

In our previous lesson—*"Free Your Spirit"*—we began to explore the true nature of the *Alpha-Spirit*, or the *actual Self*, as a *Spiritual Awareness* capable of experiencing existence from any *viewpoint*. That we seem to have fixed our *attention* and total *consideration* of our own *Beingness* solely as the *"Human Condition"* is unfortunate. But, it does not have to be permanent.

Early on our *Spiritual Timeline*—or our sense of personal "history" as an *Alpha-Spirit* (that we often refer to as the *"Backtrack"*)—we are *knowingly* acting as an *"Eternal Being"* with seemingly infinite creative abilities. This is when we were the *most* at *"Cause"* over our own *Beingness*, our *creations*, and our experience of *existence*.

Of course, being at *Cause* means also *doing* or *creating* things that one may later regret. This starts a chain of *inhibition* toward future *action* and *creation*. By experiencing *guilt* or *shame*, an individual may even begin to *hold-back* their *communication* with others. Accumulated *fragmentation* like this in specific areas led to an *Alpha-Spirit* restricting its own *active abilities* and *willingness* to *reach*—increasingly *withdrawing*, as *Cause*.

In *Systemology Level-2*, our *systematic processing* emphasis is on *"doing things"*—which is to say, the *things we have done*. It is only after the area of *"doing things"* is *confronted* easily, that we systematically consider additional matters of *ethics*, *justification* and *responsibility*.

When this subject is initially raised, the first things you might think of concern only the most serious crimes and conceptions of *"evil."* But that is only one small part of our *spiritual rehabilitation*.

The truth is that once we begin to *hold-back* or *inhibit* certain areas (or *channels*) reactively or on automatic, we stop *knowingly* being at *Cause* for that entire area—and we may even miss out on experiencing the "good things" there too.

BASIC PROCESSING

We begin this lesson by digging right in: peeling back layers of what we may easily *recall* and *consider*, much as we did for the general area of *"communication"* in earlier lessons. The goal is to again *"break through"* various *barriers* of *fragmentation* that inhibits a *Seeker's* free *consideration* and *willingness*.

In later *processing levels*, we are more concerned with what an individual considers they *"should"* or *"shouldn't"* do—or else, what you ultimately decide *to do* in the future. But before this may be experienced in *Self-honesty*, the *fragmented inhibition* that underlies free *consideration* about *action* must be handled (or rather, *defragmented*).

For *systematic processing*: we are concerned with *"spotting"* (*identifying* and *noticing* something about) a particular *action*, and then observing if there is any particular *"resistance"* to thinking about it, or any emotional *"turbulence"* attached to *considerations* of that *action*.

On a higher-level of application, the *Pathway-to-Ascension* is a progressive *"rehabilitation"* of the native or original *spiritual ability* of the individual (*Seeker, &tc.*) who

IS the *"Alpha-Spirit"* themselves. But being wrapped up in many layers and lifetimes worth of *restrictive fragmentation* inhibits true *Knowingness* of that state.

When this *Level* of *processing* is first introduced in *Traditional Piloting*, the *Seeker* is not required to give a verbal "answer" to a specific *"processing command-line"* (or "PCL") if they are uncomfortable in doing so. In this case, they simply acknowledge that they have *considered* an *answer*.

In *Systemology Level-2*, a *Seeker* may benefit from starting off *Flying-Solo*, and then *processing* any remaining *turbulent fragmentation* with *Traditional Piloting*. As usual, we will start off with light *processes* to open up the areas we will handle throughout this lesson.

Each PCL series (below) is cycled through multiple times as a complete *process*. To *run* these most effectively, a continuing *Seeker/student* should apply what they have learned about *systematic processing* in earlier lessons that included similarly-styled *processes*.

Willingness to Do
1. *"What would you be willing to do?"*
2. *"What would you be willing to have someone do?"*
3. *"What would you be willing to have others do?"*

Willingness to Reveal
1. *"What would you be willing to reveal?"*
2. *"What would you be willing to have someone reveal?"*
3. *"What would you be willing to have others reveal?"*

A *Seeker* may *run* the following process *Solo*, recording the data on paper (to see it "external" from *Self*), but then destroying (burning) it afterward. This allows a *Seeker* to *run* it without "worrying someone will find out" (which, itself, is another matter taken up later on).

A. *"What shouldn't others know about you?"*

B. *"Who would it be safe to communicate that to?"*

C. *"What shouldn't someone know about others?"*

D. *"Who would it be safe to communicate that to?"*

Once this area has been approached as a general area, *processing* may then be directly applied to various "*terminals*" ("persons," "places," "things," *&tc*). As a standard, we start by *processing* basic *terminals* that represent each of the "*Spheres of Existence*" (introduced in *Lesson 2* of the "*Basic Course*"). These include: "YOUR BODY"; "A FAMILY MEMBER"; "CHILDREN"; "SEX"; "WORK"; "SOCIETY"; "LIFE ON EARTH"; "PHYSICAL MATTER"; and "THOUGHT" (or "SPIRITS"). On additional (advanced) passes through this course material later on, consider also "CREATION" and "DESTRUCTION."

The "*terminals*" (given above) are general examples. Other similar (but more specific) *terminals* with *turbulent fragmentation* may be used in place of them. For example: "A HUSBAND" (for "Family Member"), "HOUSEKEEPING" (for "Work"), or "AN AUTOMOBILE" (for "Physical Matter").

This *processing formula* includes several individual *processes* that are used together to form a complete *routine* for *running* a particular *terminal* in this area of "*doing things.*" A *routine* such as this is preferably handled within a single *session*. Insert the "terminal name" into the following *formula*:

A1. *"What have you done involving ---?"*

A2. *"What have you held-back from doing involving ---?"*

B1. *"What has someone else, or others, done involving ---?"*

B2. *"What has someone else, or others, held-back from doing involving ---?"*

C1. *"What would you permit someone, or others, to do involving ---?"*

C2. *"What have you kept someone else, or others, from doing involving ---?"*

D1. *"What could you permit others to find out about you involving ---?"*

D2. *"What have you held-out from communicating about ---?"*

E1. *"What could someone, or others, let you find out about themselves involving ---?"*

E2. *"What have others held-out from communicating about ---?"*

The "ultimate" *process* for this area is *run* after *all* previous *processing* given in this section. It does not apply "terminals"; it assists with stabilizing results and/or prompting *end-point realizations* for this level of *processing* as a whole.

A1. *"What have you done?"*

A2. *"What have you held-back from doing?"*

B1. *"What has someone else (or others) done?"*

B2. *"What has someone else (or others) held-back from doing?"*

C1. *"What would you permit someone (or others) to do?"*

C2. *"What have you kept someone (or others) from doing?"*

D1. *"What could you permit someone (or others) to find out about you?"*

D2. *"What have you held-out from communicating?"*

E1. *"What could someone (or others) let you find out about them?"*

E2. *"What have others held-out from communicating?"*

PROCESSING "INVALIDATION"

Ultimately, at the basic core of the matter, *abilities* of an *Alpha-Spirit* can only be weakened or "lost" by their own decision. These kind of decisions are sometimes known as *"postulates"* or *Alpha-Thought*. They are the *Alpha-Spirit's* prime decision for something *"to be"* or *"not-be"* what it *Is*. This includes an individual's own *Beingness*, their own "sense" of *Self*—and decisions about what *"Self"* ultimately *Is*.

Although the *actual decision* rests with *Self*, there are many ways in which an *Alpha-Spirit* might be influenced to make such decisions. In order for *Self* to *Be* "less" than what *Self* actually is (in its true native state), it must, by definition, be *"invalidated."*

The originating trigger or restimulation of *"invalidation fragmentation"* is usually from someone else, or others. It is only when these criticisms or opinions are, for whatever reason, actually *agreed* to as *reality* (made "one's own") from a higher-level of thought (or *postulate*) that they will affect *Self* (the *Alpha-Spirit*).

This *fragmentation* prompts an individual to start *validating* the *invalidation* and therefore make it "true" for their experience of existence (or *reality*). In common terms: it becomes a *"self-fulfilling prophecy"* of sorts. The individual now *fully* "*believes*" themselves *to be* "incapable" of an *ability*, and so essentially becomes so.

The proper way to develop, enhance, or regain, an ability, requires *validating* one's own successes—even when they are only small gains. Eventually, we want to be able to withstand *invalidation* from other outside sources as well; to *confront* their existence without *agreeing* to them ourselves. An *actualized* individual could face all the criticism in the world and be unaffected so long as they do not consider *Self* as "*less*."

A professional may make many mistakes, but the skill level increases when these are not used to *invalidate* the many accomplishments that have taken place along the way. A professional in sports continues their improvement by *validating* the many goals, hits, or scores, they have made in their career. They do not *invalidate* themselves just because of a critical miss—in spite of the "boos" and ridicule from others.

In a state of *fragmentation*—outside *Self-Honesty*—the *Human Condition* maintains a quite "fragile" sense of *Self-worth* and *certainty*. The less *actualized* an individual is, the more easily their thought processes and actions may become "unbalanced"; the more easily they may be led to *invalidate* whatever slight confidence they have. Our goal is not to run from or avoid *invalidation*, but to emphasize *validation* of the "good."

On our long journey down the *Backtrack* of existence, we have experienced a great many things on *both* sides of this area—and hence our *processing* must treat *considerations* derived from *both* sides: because we have all participated in *invalidating* each other at some point or another. This even led us to being more susceptible to its *effects*, ourselves.

One reason we do not want to act in "avoidance" of *invalidation*, is because operating in such a manner often includes "*holding-back*" as a mechanism. To avoid any possibility of *invalidation*, or situations where one may encounter it, the individual holds themselves back from reaching into entire areas of existence.

The following two basic *processes* are *run* to explore *considerations* on the subject of *invalidation*.

A1. "*How could you avoid invalidation?*"
A2. "*How could you attract invalidation?*"

B1. "*How could someone else (or others) avoid invalidation?*"
B2. "*How could someone else (or others) attract invalidation?*"

This next *process* applies "*analytical recall*" to the "*circuits.*"

1. "*Recall invalidating someone.*"
2. "*Recall being invalidated.*"
3A. "*Recall someone else invalidating another (or others).*"
3B. "*Recall someone else invalidating themselves.*"
0. "*Recall invalidating yourself.*"

Now we apply a combination of traditional "*New Thought*" and *Systemology* to start handling specifics. The first PCL is:

A. "*What might you be invalidated for?*"

Once the *Seeker* has an "answer" that may be *processed*, the following two PCL are *run* until some sense of "relief" or "release" is experienced. Then use the first PCL (above) to locate and *run* another *invalidation*. "*Invalidation*" means "making less of." In this *process*, we are focusing on *imagining* the "opposite" of *invalidation* taking place: *validating* an individual's true *Spiritual Beingness* as they are (or appear to be).

B. "*Imagine someone else validating you for having it.*"

C. "*Imagine someone else having a similar disability or weakness; then imagine yourself validating them for having it.*"

Running processes for the conceptual areas of "*criticism*" and "*judgment*" is closely related to "*invalidation*." Therefore, consider tolerable "*acceptance*" and "*rejection*" for *all three areas*. These may be run consecutively (one after another, each concept applied as its own *process*). Use the concepts of "INVALIDATION"; "CRITICISM"; and "JUDGMENT" to complete the PCL below. [This "acceptance/rejection" style of *systematic processing* is introduced in *Lesson-4* of this series.]

A. "*What --- could you accept?*"

B. "*What --- could you reject?*"

"HOSTILE-ACTS" & "HOLD-OUTS"

An entire volume of the *Systemology Core*, titled "*Way of the Wizard*," is dedicated to the subject of "*ethics*." In this present *Professional Course* series, we simplify the subject and emphasize only what directly pertains to *processing*. It is necessary for completing "*Systemology Level-2*." It is not, however, an area that many *Seekers* particularly enjoy—and thus we begin to see some of them fall by the wayside of the *Pathway* around this point of progression.

The development and use of our *Systemology* is possible so late in the "*game*" of our *Spiritual Existence*, because we have only now been able and willing to fully *observe* and *understand* the patterns of our *thoughts*, *behaviors*, and ultimately the *roles* that we play out, in each consecutive experience of a lifetime. Some of what we have experienced is difficult to "face"—difficult to *confront* "*As-It-Is*"—and yet, without doing so, we restrict ourselves from having total access to our own *Cosmic History*.

In actual truth, as *Spiritual Beings*, we have been involved in *games* of "conflict" and "domination" for a very long time. We have experienced, again, *both sides* of most everything by this point in our existence—even if we have *blocked-out* or *blacked-out* much of this memory. But memory exists in "sequences" and "chains"—and our unwillingness to *confront* something, *blocks-out* entire areas of *Knowingness* and *ability*.

We take a systematic approach to considering the mechanisms that are attached to committing a *Harmful-Act*, which is to say, an action that directly harms *someone* else —or some other "*Sphere of Existence*." This is an important area to *process* prior to any higher-level *considerations* of "*ethics*" or "*moral justification*."

A *Hostile-Act* or *Harmful-Act* is the start of a systematic sequence that generally results in *fragmentation*. First, there is the "act" or "action" itself. Then, the mind naturally considers "*motivation*" for that action and others similar to it. For example: when one is struck by another, there is a tendency to want to "*balance*" that action, and one *considers* that they have a "*motivation*" to strike back.

To extend this example: an individual is likely to claim that the "harm" *they have done* is "*motivated*" by the "harm" *done to them*. The *Alpha-Spirit* begins to "*postulate*" this as *reality*; the Mind-System follows by correcting its *perceptions* accordingly. But, by this insistence on manifesting a "balance" of "harm" we find the individual getting entangled in a *Spirit-Trap* that it didn't see coming.

Some traditions recognize a *karma*-like mechanism at play in the Universe. In most cases, however, this is usually considered as something mediated by an "outside" or "other-determined" source. The actual fact is that we impose this *karma* upon our own *reality*. And it systematically plays out like this:

Our insistence that harm "must be" balanced then leaves us with our own "unmotivated" *Harmful-Acts* that "must be" balanced by *future* "motivators." This means receiving harm in the *future* that one feels they, themselves, deserve (to balance what they have done). What's more: having committed a *Harmful-Act*, the individual starts to "*hold-out*" (*withdraw*) their communication with various individuals, groups, or even entire areas of existence.

This whole "systematic" sequence may be taking place quite *unknowingly*, because the original "*postulate*" for such automated-mechanisms to exist were put into "play" by *Self* as a *reality-agreement* long ago. But before we begin *processing* these areas, let us consider how an individual gets entangled in such *Spirit-Traps* in the first place.

"SPIRIT-TRAPS" AND "REALITY"

The subjects of *"Reality"* and *"Existence"* are approached somewhat indirectly all along the *Pathway-to-Ascension*. Our understanding of what *Is*, and the nature of our own participation with *Reality*, improves cumulatively the whole way.

Participation in this *Shared Universe* is quite similar to our experiences of the many that preceded it. This *Reality* is a "shared illusion" *created* by the *Alpha-Spirit*—the individual themselves—that is experiencing it. This is always the case, even before an *Alpha-Spirit* "shared" their *created illusions* with others, and simply *created* in isolation for one's own *Self* as a personal "Home Universe."

Although the *Alpha-Spirit* is the ultimate *creator* of their own *Reality*, there is a separation or fragmentation inherent from the beginning in order to experience that *created reality* or "illusion." Without this separation, an individual would have "total identification" with their *creation*; and in a *Shared Universe*, it would result in a "total identification" with everyone else. There would be no sense of "individuality"; there would also be no continuation of a "growth-pattern" left unattended.

Communication is an underlying factor in establishing and maintaining *reality-agreements* concerning a *Shared Universe*. To maintain "individuality" we must see the whole as a system fragmented into parts, which may then communicate with each other across a perceived distance. The continuous experience of any *Reality* (or *Universe*) is maintained by the continuous communication among those *sharing* it.

In the most material sense, *communication* is a motion, action, or relay, of a particle (or data) from a *source-point* to a *receipt-point*, across some distance of space. It is such motion that gives us a sense of *"sequential time,"* but that is not our present concern. What we are concerned with is the fact that a communication means, in essence, *duplicating* or *copying* something at a *receipt-point* the same as it exists at the *source-point*.

What we consider *"Existence"* or a *Universe* is really the continuous communication of *reality-agreements* among all those concerned. Each individual is essentially *creating* and *duplicating* the communication from their own *viewpoint*, within their own *Personal Universe*. The level or degree of actual *duplication* is reflected in the level or degree of "synchronous exchange" (or "sameness") experienced by all those sharing it.

In previous lessons, we have treated "communication" as spoken messages; but it is also reflected in the "actions" one takes with others and their environment. Actions *are* communications. They involve a relay of intention; and they are governed by the same element of *willingness* that affects our *reach* and *withdraw* in other areas of life, and in other forms of communication.

Duplication is a critical component of a *Shared Universe*. In terms of communicated action: let us consider that whether you "hug" or "harm" an individual, at some level, there is a *"mental image"* of that *reality* (and a *duplication* of it) communicated and shared between all parties (or *"terminals"*) involved.

What we essentially mean here is that: in a *Shared Universe* (or *Reality*), an individual *Alpha-Spirit* is still *creating* from within their own *Personal Universe*. However, those *creations* now include a *duplication* of shared experiences. Both the *source*-role and *effect*-role are *created* as a *reality* within the *Personal Universe* of each individual *sharing* the interaction (or communication).

In light of this, a *Seeker* may better understand why there is an emphasis on "circuits" in *systematic processing*. We are *creating*—albeit *duplicating*—and *recording data* for *all* interacting *viewpoints* (*Personal Universes* of other *Spiritual Beings*) of a shared experience as part of our own *reality* (our own *Personal Universe*).

An *Alpha-Spirit* is already experiencing some degree of *fragmentation knowingly* by engaging in a *Shared Universe*. This is what allows for a simultaneous *"individual"* and *"shared"* experience. The *duplication factor* allows one to get a sense of, or feel, *both* sides of a communication— and even to *duplicate* the "opposite" role. This only works out for our benefit when interactions are those that are desirable to *both* parties.

We are in constant interaction—or communication—with others and our environment every day of our earthly lives. *Imprinting* from all of these interactions is not necessarily *persistently* and *compulsively created* as part of our more permanent *reality-agreements*, and therefore may not all be a significant source of *spiritual fragmentation*. The primary factor on this is what we are *knowingly willing* to *confront* and *accept*.

"Do unto others..." has existed as a *"Golden Rule"* for thousands of years, but failed to perfect the *Human Condition*. We are interested in the entire experience from someone else's *viewpoint*, in addition to the actions themselves. It is not a matter of whether you would like it or *accept* it from your own *viewpoint*, but whether you would like (or *accept*) it from the *viewpoint* of the *effect*-role (the "other person"), meaning *them* (as the individual *they* are).

The real *fragmentation* begins to accumulate (and *Awareness* is increasingly entangled) when an individual becomes *unwilling* to experience the *effect* they have *created* —meaning, of course, *unwilling* to *confront* the *viewpoint* of the opposing-role. Keep in mind that we are, again, referring to something that an individual is *unwilling* to *confront* and experience, that they themselves are *creating* (or *duplicating*) as *reality* for their own *Personal Universe.* And therein lies the rudiments of a *trap* for the *Awareness* of an *Alpha-Spirit.*

SOME BASIC TECHNIQUES

To start off lightly in the areas we have been discussing, alternate the following PCL:

A. "*Recall a time that was pleasant for both you and someone else.*"

B. "*Imagine the experience from their viewpoint.*"

Using the above *process* as an example, place an emphasis (for "Step-B") on "getting a sense of" or "feeling" things from other people's *viewpoints*. This may also be practiced as an "*objective process*" when engaging in pleasant social interactions. The goal is to "*imagine*" or "*duplicate*" the senses or impressions perceived from another *viewpoint*. For example: how *you* might look or sound to *someone else* as you talk to them.

When we speak of *Harmful-Acts*, we mean when someone else was harmed. It does not matter what the circumstances for it are—whether intentional or accidental, whether in *Self-defense* or even to protect others; if you are *unwilling* to *confront* the action, an experience of its *effects* may be waiting in your future.

In *systematic processing*, such *effects* may be *"run out"* (or *"processed out"*) so that an individual is no longer *unknowingly* and *continuously* maintaining that *fragmentation* on their ongoing *"life-track."* The most basic solution is simply to *knowingly confront* things in *processing* by using *imagined* representations.

Much of this *"karmic" fragmentation* lies dormant for long periods of time, which is why we seldom will experience any instantaneous "repercussion" of our actions. The "balancing" *effects* generally manifest at times and in ways that are quite far and removed from the original *imprinting incident*. As a result, this "mechanism" is not even an effective "learning tool" to properly steer an individual to a higher ethics.

As we begin to *process* more specific or direct examples, it is best to start with lighter experiences. In this case, we want to locate (or "spot") a specific instance in memory where you caused someone else harm. It does not have to be a particularly significant *Harmful-Act* at first, but should be something which you later regretted—such as "hurting someone else's feelings," *&tc*.

The most basic method of *confronting* the action is to *imagine* the experience from the other person's *viewpoint*; and getting a sense for how they felt at the time. In order to achieve any kind of "release" or "relief" from this exercise, you may need to alternate between the *viewpoints*: first spotting your actions from your own *viewpoint*, then spotting the event and sensations experienced from the other *viewpoint*.

If this *process* makes things seem more "heavy" or "solid"—as opposed to a sense of "relief"—then it is likely that any *turbulence* or *fragmentation* is tied strongly to a similar type of incident that happened prior to it. If this earlier incident can be located, then the same *process* (above) is applied to *that* action or event.

In the case of a *Harmful-Act* where the "victim" was not present (such as "vandalism," *&tc.*), a *Seeker* would "*imagine*" the scenario (and "feelings") that the other person *might* have experienced upon its discovery. Progressively work your way through whatever is easily recalled for this first pass through the materials.

While we have emphasized "out-flow" (Circuit-1) of the *Harmful-Act* itself, remember that *all viewpoints* are *duplicated* from an *imprinting incident*. This means that a "victim" may also "pull in" (Circuit-2) *fragmentation* of the opposing-role (and its "karma") as their own *reality*, by also not *confronting* it "*As-It-Is.*" This is what causes individuals to "*dramatize*" (or "act out to others") what has been *done to* them.

The same techniques (previously described) are applied, but this time *running* the *processes* by *imagining* the "attackers" *viewpoint* as they commit the *Harmful-Act*. This sometimes stirs up more *emotional turbulence* than when treating one's own actions (Circuit-1). In this case, a "relief" or "release" point occurs when a *Seeker* can easily *confront* the action without any particular *compulsive* desire to do it themselves.

ESCAPING THE TRAPS

It is important to note that these *"karmic"* mechanisms that we speak of are *not* the *only* reason that things happen. Just because someone acts against you does not mean you automatically deserved it as some kind of long-running tab of retribution. And while all "actions" have a certain *cause* and *sequence* behind them, everything that happens is *not* you pulling some cosmic destiny in on your reality. Things can *just* happen.

However, if there *is* a particularly *turbulent* area that persists in spite of your basic efforts (as given in the previous sections) to *confront* it *"As-It-Is,"* then this "trap-type" of *fragmentation* may indeed be (at least partly) *"in play."*

When *processing* these areas—particularly when *Flying-Solo*—it is preferred to focus on the *out-flows* (Circuit-1) regarding what *you have done*, because the greatest gains are achieved when *processing* toward *"being* at *cause."* Of course, a *Seeker* must also *confront in-flows* or what has been *done to them* (Circuit-2); but *running* this too long (without an alternation with *out-flows*) will tend to overemphasize *"being* at *effect."*

The goal of *Systemology Level-2* (in combination with *processing* from previous *levels*) is for a *Seeker* to release themselves from the heavier "energetic burdens" that they carry as a *Spiritual Being*—that which is most accessible to *process* at this stage of the *Pathway*. We mean, of course, the "unraveling" or "dissolving" of *energetic-masses* that entangle an individual's *Spiritual Awareness* into the fixed solidity of *fragmentation*.

"Withholding" things is one way our *Awareness* becomes entangled and unavailable to us. By this, we don't necessarily mean simply not saying or doing something; but when *attention* must be actively applied in order to *restrain* one's *Self* from such, then we are *"holding-back"* our *Self (unknowingly)* in other ways too.

A *"hold-back"* on action and ability generally begins with a *"hold-out"* on communication. An example of this might be to *"hold-out"* on one's true opinion of something in order to spare someone else's feelings. Another might be to *"hold-out"* sharing something that would be socially inappropriate or unacceptable. Finally, and most critically, there is what we *"hold-out"* communicating out of guilt or fear of punishment.

In a *Shared Universe*, all of these are examples where an individual goes *"out-of-communication"* with other *"terminals"* and *"Spheres of Existence."* As demonstrated throughout the previous lessons of this *Professional Course* series, this is the first factor that leads to increased *fragmentation* and various difficulties maintaining true *Self-determinism* and a *Self-Honest* experience of existence.

As an exercise in *processing out-flow*, the standard practice in *Mardukite Zuism* and the *Systemology Society* is for a *Seeker* to write "confessional letters" (while alone)—to see the events as separate from *Self*—and then immediately burn them. The practice of "confessing to another" (in *Traditional Piloting*) *does* have spiritual value, but it can also be easily abused or mishandled (and is not covered in this present lesson).

If the "confessional letter" does not provide a sense of "relief" or "release" with a particular incident, terminal or area, there is another factor that may be involved.

The *turbulence* attached to various *Harmful-Acts* increases with the amount of *attention* that an individual places on it "internally" to "keep it in check" (so to speak). This is most critical with those things we worry about *"someone finding out."* A lot of *Awareness* is suspended or fixated on *those* things—and that intense "internalization" of our *attention-energy* also has a tendency to "pull-in" a lot of what we "don't want" in our lives.

One of the reasons this area is so critical is that: similar to how the *fragmentation* of an *"imprint"* might be restimulated by a certain *"facet"* in our environment, the *energetic-turbulence* associated with a *Harmful-Act* may be stirred up reactively (automatically) when someone *almost* discovers one of our *"hold-outs."*

This "fear of discovery" causes *attention* to "invigorate" or "validate" that area again with more of our *Awareness*. And this is generally instigated or caused by an "outside" *other-determined* source. The solution is to *confront* the thing *"As-It-Is"* with high-powered *Awareness* in *processing* on one's own determination, rather than *withdrawing* from it and feeding it with low-level *attention* each time it gets restimulated.

We address this now at our present gradient of the *Pathway* because: should anything similar to what we are describing get restimulated in any *processing*, it must be handled (with *processing*) before any stable gains or further progress is possible. The simple fact that some "thing" *suddenly appears* in *processing* generally means it is a source of *fragmentation* that requires getting under one's own *Self*-control.

REACHING FURTHER

This lesson marks the completion of *Systemology Level-2*. This is a critical checkpoint on the *Pathway* for *Seekers*. This is also a point where a *Seeker* might cycle back to the beginning of these *Professional Course* lessons and *process* their way through a second pass of all the materials presented up until now.

Although the written materials (for this level) may end here, the point to which a *Seeker* can reach with the existing *processing* given may not have been attained with their first pass.

Ideally, a *Seeker* that has fully completed *Systemology Level-2* will have a much greater and more stable certainty on "*Being* an *Alpha-Spirit* that is *having* a *Human* experience." This certainty should be at such a level as to prevent a *Seeker* from being so easily "trapped" in the "problems" of the *Human Condition* ever again.

By this, we do not mean that a *Seeker* will have completely "broken free" of the *Human Condition* at this juncture of the *Pathway*. They are still likely to experience some emotional fluctuation with daily life. But, they are not likely to become so deeply entangled in it; they have a better understanding of how the *Human* "game" is played in this world—and how to handle it well enough to continue their progress on the *Pathway*.

The final exercise given for this *processing level* should assist with these goals. It covertly emphasizes that you—as an *Alpha-Spirit*—are not *actually* "located" *anywhere*. It is simply part of our "*game*" in this existence—to *pretend* to "be" in the "locations" from which we *perceive* or *operate*.

The PCL for this exercise is:

"Close your eyes; spot places where you are not. Spot many places."

We say that our goal is "covertly" embedded in the PCL, because by "checking" that you are "not" somewhere, you tend to put *attention* on it to *look* at it—thereby transferring (or "projecting" if you prefer) some degree of personal *Awareness* to that location (which is "*exterior*" from the "*body*").

The PCL does not limit *where* these "places" are. They are "spotted" by *attention* with eyes closed; they do not need to be considered relatively "nearby." This practice is repeated until some sense of *exterior* "ZU-Vision" is achieved. At this *processing level*, these perceptions do not have to be very vivid or accurate, so long as a *Seeker* feels they have achieved an "improved" or "increased" sense of this spiritual ability.

LESSON SEVEN: ELIMINATING BARRIERS

GAMES AND BARRIERS

Participation in, and experience of, the Physical Universe (*"Beta Existence"*) is likened to a *"game"* in our *Systemology*. For philosophical and practical purposes, we apply *game theory* concepts to our *systematic processing* with regards to a *Seeker's* experience of *"Universes."* As such, an intellectual pursuit into *game theory* is of increasing interest to a *Seeker* as they progress along the *Pathway* (particularly at upper levels).

Perhaps the first thing that you should know about *"games"* is that they consist of certain "rules" or *"reality-agreements"* in order to functionally exist. In addition to an assigned *"space"* or *"game-field"* (or else, a *Shared Universe*) there are very specific *considerations* that define the *reality* of *"abilities"* (or *"freedoms"*) and *"purposes"* (or *"goals"*).

Reality-Agreements also define the *"barriers"* (*boundaries* and *obstacles*) that allow us to actually *have* a *game*. Unlimited freedom; no game. Unlimited barriers; no game. A lack of any purposes or goals; no game. So, for us to *have* any sense of a *"game"* in our lives, there are ultimately *"barriers"* in place that affect (or restrict, on an apparent level) our perceived *freedom* of play—meaning our *abilities* and *Knowingness*.

An *Alpha-Spirit* participates in *games* because it is something to *do*. We have all existed for a very long span of perceived *time* and have experienced countless different *Universes* along the way. We have also all *played* countless different *"roles"* during the course of our *Spiritual Exist-*

ence; made decisions based on perceived *"goals"* in each of these lifetimes. All of these aspects are considered within the domain of our *game theory*.

While our application of *game theory* reoccurs frequently in later *processing levels*, our present concern (when first entering *Systemology Level-3*) is specifically the subject of *barriers*. This lesson directly continues from the material given in the previous one, and its invitation for a *Seeker* to *"reach further."* We will begin with some *"upper-level" Systemology philosophy*.

FRAGMENTATION AND BARRIERS

When first engaging in *Shared Universes* (or *Games Universes*), an *Alpha-Spirit* "agrees" to the *"reality"* of certain *barriers* in order to participate in and experience a specific *"Game of Life."* These *"reality-agreements"* make the *barriers* seem more *solid* than they *actually* are, and seem more *real* than the very *agreements* and *considerations* themselves that compose them.

During one's lifetime, an individual gets to believing that there are even more *barriers* than there are—and this is even the *esoteric* basis for dividing our perception of *ALL-Existence* into a series of *"veils"* or *"gates."* For example: an individual believes they cannot *perceive, know,* or even *think* about certain things, because it somehow *"goes beyond"* or *"exceeds"* a certain *barrier*—even though that *barrier* does not actually exist.

Fragmented and low-*Awareness* states (that are typical of the *Human Condition*) allow an individual to falsely believe that the *barriers* and other *"game-mechanics"* are superior (or more solid/real) than the *agreements* and *considerations*; but *"games"* and *"barriers"* are really a "product of" *thoughts*. The *agreements* that compose the observable solidity of this *Universe* are really just a matter of "convenience" in order for us to have any kind of "shared" *reality* with others that are also experiencing this *Universe*.

The *"mechanics"* are simply solidified *"reality-agreements"* that provide an internal logic or consistent pattern for the *game* or *Universe*. Otherwise, consider three friends walking down a road: spontaneously, one turns into a tree; one disappears into a black-hole; and one simply sinks through the pavement, right through the earth, and into outer-space. Such *"randomness"* does not manifest on this planet because of agreed-upon *game-mechanics* inherent in the makeup and design of *this* specific *Universe* ("*Beta-Existence*").

We *agreed* to the *game-mechanics* (and the *barriers*) so long ago that we have forgotten about it. *Fragmentation* leads us to believe that we are completely under the *effect* of these *"mechanics"*—and that this *Physical Universe* (or *Beta-Existence*) is somehow superior to our own true existence as *Alpha-Spirits*, when it is not.

But, these original *reality-agreements* were *"postulated"* into *existence* from a higher-level of *"Alpha-Thought."* They become quite solid by comparison to the level of *thought* and *consideration* available to the standard-issue *Human Condition*, which generally operates from a *viewpoint* "below" the level of those *agreements*. Thus, the "power" of *Human Thought* does not produce the same solid level of *effect* on one's environment.

It becomes quite apparent (from within our philosophy)

that *fragmentation*, itself, is the only *real barrier*—and it is all that allows an *Alpha-Spirit* to get overwhelmed (or overpowered) by *Beta-Existence*, and believe *Self* to *be* something less than it actually is. This is what restricts an *Alpha-Spirit's* freedom and ability to fully "act" *within* the framework of the *game-mechanics*, when *Self* created and agreed to them in the first place.

In a state of *fragmentation*—such as the *Human Condition*—relatively "newer" *considerations* have less impact on the *mechanics* of the apparent *"Objective Universe"* than those *reality-agreements* made as *"Alpha-Thought."* The "original" *agreements* are more "solid" in their apparent *reality* than "newer" *beliefs* and *considerations*. It is in this wise that an *Alpha-Spirit* became the *effect* of their own *creations*.

When an individual *"thinks"* or *"considers"* from a *viewpoint* within the *Human Condition*, they are running up against the very *game-mechanics* of *Beta-Existence*—and by this we mean very specifically: the high-level *agreements* an *Alpha-Spirit* has formerly made about *space-time* and *energy-matter* in this *Physical Universe*.

Some of the most basic *systematic processing* techniques (such as the *"objective processing"* exercises found throughout this *course* and in a *Formal Session*) are strongly effective because they put a *Seeker* into such *clear communication* with the *Physical Universe* that they can more easily reclaim the *certainty, spiritual power,* and *creative ability* of their own original *"Alpha-Thought"* (*agreements* and *postulates*).

What is described within this section of our lesson is essentially the actual theory behind "opening procedures" and various techniques for establishing "presence in-session" used in formal *processing*.

For example: when a *Seeker* repeatedly (and *knowingly*) *"looks at"* and *"contacts the solidity"* of a *wall* that is in front of them with total *Awareness*, they *really "see"* the *wall* that *is* there *"As-It-Is"* (and often for the first time). [Refer to *Lesson-1 "Increasing Awareness,"* section titled: *"The Wall."*]

In essence, there is an "upper-level" *realization* available that *Self* has *created*, and is *agreeing* to, the *mechanics* of the *barrier* on a continuous and compulsive basis. Once this is *recognized*, a *Seeker* can then begin to practice regaining the true "power" behind their *considerations*, and again have any high-level *control* (*"Alpha-Thought"*) over the actual *reality-agreements* and *mechanics* of a *Universe*.

PROCESSING "BARRIERS"

The *mechanics* of a *Shared/Game Universe* become such a point of inherent personal *fragmentation* that they act as apparent (or even visible) *"barriers"*—at least until the individual is again *able* to *be* free of them. It is not the *agreement* to have *barriers* and *games* that is problematic; the *fragmentation* occurs when the *Alpha-Spirit* is no longer *aware* of these *agreements*, yet continues to compulsively maintain their *reality*.

There are many times when it seems like certain applications of *systematic processing* shouldn't be necessary, since it should not be altogether difficult to "change your mind" about things. And if we could easily get an individual (entrapped within the *Human Condition*) to *actual-*

ly "change their mind" at an upper-level of *Alpha-Thought*, then indeed, *processing* wouldn't be necessary. But that is not the general experience of *Life*.

Systematic Processing is intended to assist a *Seeker* in eliminating the *barriers* of their own "*blindness*" or "*spiritual occlusion*"—meaning their *unreality* or *unknowingness* on the *reality-agreements* they've previously *agreed* to.

In the end: a *fragmented individual* is working against themselves in this *Universe*—working against their own former *agreements*. This only furthers the *solidity* of, and entrapment of a personal *viewpoint* within, this *Universe*. Using *force* against *force*, *energy* against *energy*, only strengthens the *reality* of this *existence*; whereas true *Alpha-Thought* requires no "*force*" or "*energy*" to "*postulate/create*" something into being.

Our previous example regarding our "*wall*" exercise is quite apt, because it also represents a "*physical barrier.*" After making *agreements* for the *reality* of *solid-matter* and a dependency on *viewpoints* attached to *physical eyes* (of a *body*), the *wall* represents a *barrier* to the total potential freedoms available. This is what makes receiving accurate *perceptions* from "*remote*" *viewpoints* (ZU-Vision) difficult for those individuals that continue to *compulsively create* and *unknowingly agree* to the *reality* of the *wall* as a *real barrier* for *Self*.

There are other *agreed-upon barriers* of a *Shared Universe* as well, less obvious perhaps, such as "*space*"—which is also to say "*distance.*" And if there is to be any *creation* or *activity* within this "*space,*" then there is also the observable factor of "*time*"—particularly when there is a perceived *motion* across "*distances*" (or even inherently in the "decay" or "erosion" of what is considered *solid-matter*).

For example: *communication* is a relay or motion of a "particle" or "bit" from "*Spot-A*" to "*Spot-B*." It must "*cross a distance*" and thus there is some "*time-lag*" in this action. It would be instantaneous were it not for the perception of some kind of *barrier*, such as *distance*. Without a *spatial distance*, however, there would be no "*Spot-A*" or "*Spot-B*" since the two would be indistinguishable and now essentially the same "spot."

There is a systematic relationship between *communication* and "*proximity*" (or "*closeness*"). This is reflected in the degree of "*likingness*" or "*affinity*" that is shared between ourselves and other individuals and things.

What we "*like*," we generally want to keep "*closer*" to us; and the more we engage in *true communication* with someone, the more we can get to *liking* them, come into *closer* "*agreement*" with them (and be even further inclined to *communicate* with them more). We are, of course, only describing a systematic tendency in this case, not an absolute.

But these "factors" of *communication*, *likingness* and *agreement* are indeed interconnected; and that is how the area of "*barriers*" is initially handled at this *systematic processing level*. What is "*fragmentation*," but an *energetic-mass*; and what is an "*energetic-mass*," in an otherwise clear flow or current, but a "*barrier*."

For training and demonstration purposes, it may be helpful to *imagine* these *three factors* as a "current-flow" or "channel" connected between all individuals and things in existence. The "degree," "type," or "intensity" of these *flows* tends to rise or fall collectively. Individuals *communicate*, they *like* each other, and *agree* with each other, *&tc.*, or else they "break," "reject," or otherwise "wall up" against these connections.

It is true that we may initially have "good reason" for establishing *"breaks"* and *"barriers."* However, we also have that interrelationship of factors (*communication, likingness,* and *agreement*) to be concerned with. This means by "cutting" *communication,* one then deals with *dislike* and *disagreement, &tc.* And there is the potential for an *automatic* (or *compulsive*) continuation of a *"break"* or *"barrier" unknowingly.*

More importantly is the fact that when the "event" or "incident" that prompted the *break* is not properly *confronted "As-It-Is,"* then *fragmentation* generally ensues. This means there is a potential for *turbulent emotional* or *mental "charge"* in that entire area thereafter. And this increasingly builds up as *"chain of fragmentation"* connected to other similar "incidents."

For example: an individual that has often had their *affections* (*likingness*) "rejected" is likely to be more emotionally sensitive to that area, or more turbulently reactive at even the most subtle indications of "rejection" in the future. Our systematic solution is to handle the considerations from earlier "rejections" (which is where the primary *fragmentation* or "upset" is actually stemming from).

Breaks and *barriers* (in our three *flow-factors*) can occur from "enforcement" in addition to "rejecting" or "inhibiting" something. "Too much" of something is often just as uncomfortable as its "absence." This includes any time "too much" *force* is applied to any of our *flow-factors*—such as being *"forced to agree."* Quickly, we will shut down *communication flows*, then strongly *dislike* and *disagree* and so on as a cycle.

We say that this type of *fragmentation* occurs as a "chain" that is connected to many incidents—not just the one that *"triggered"* or *"restimulated"* a *reaction*. Usually the *reaction* is also out of "proportion" to what the present incident called for. But in essence, that is not *all* that the individual is *reacting* to; there is an entire "chain" of *fragmentation* accumulated from our past (or *"Backtrack"*) that is also now "active" and present.

The systematic solution to these types of "upsets" is to *"spot"* the underlying source of *fragmentation* that has *"resurfaced"* (or is *"in restimulation"*). This actually increases *"Actualized Awareness"* when one is "upset"—as opposed to trying to get someone to "calm down," which is really only a *"suppression"* (and which only further validates and strengthens the *fragmentation* itself).

Systematic Processing in these areas is most effective when the *earliest* incident of a certain type of occurrence can be *spotted*. For a *Seeker's* first cycle through the lessons of the *Professional Course*, only those events taking place during *this* lifetime are *processed* (unless additional data is already readily available); however, in later passes through our *course* material, an advanced application would include "past lives" (*"Backtrack"*) too.

DEFRAGMENTING THE "FACTORS"

We have, for our *systematic processing*, three "factors" (or *flow-factors*) that require *defragmentation*: *"communication,"* *"likingness"* and *"agreement."* There are also two basic *flow-types* applied to each *factor*: *"insistence"* (or *"enforcement"*) and *"rejection"* (or *"inhibition"*).

The three *processing command-lines* ("PCL") for each of the following *processes* are *run* in alternation until any sense of *"fragmented energetic charge"* (concerning an area) has fallen away or dispersed. *Run* as many of the *processes* within a single *session* as can be handled—being certain to *end-the-session* when "feeling good" and alert. All of these *processes* employ the *"Analytical Recall"* technique (as first described in *Lesson-2* of this *Professional Course*).

As an additional point of instruction: if any of the *processes* stirs up significant *energetic turbulence*, a more complete *defragmentation* will only occur if an *earlier* instance of a similar type is *spotted*. This may, in fact, have to continue "down a chain" of *even earlier* instances until the *earliest* one available for *recall* is *spotted*. Only then can the actual *fragmented imprint* (underlying the "upset") be handled and *confronted*. Also be sure to *notice* some "things" and "actions" within the incident, rather than simply listing it off as *recalled*.

Communication Factor: Enforced Out-Flows

1. *"Recall a time when you insisted that someone communicate with someone (or something)."*

2. *"Recall a time when someone insisted that you communicate with someone (or something)."*

3. *"Recall a time when someone insisted others communicate with someone (or something)."*

Communication Factor: Enforced In-Flows

1. *"Recall a time when you insisted that someone communicate with you."*

2. *"Recall a time when someone insisted that you communicate with them."*

3. *"Recall a time when someone insisted that others communicate with them."*

Communication Factor: Inhibited Out-Flows

1. *"Recall a time when you insisted that someone not communicate with someone (or something)."*

2. *"Recall a time when someone insisted that you not communicate with something (or someone)."*

3. *"Recall a time when someone insisted that others not communicate with someone (or something)."*

Communication Factor: Inhibited In-Flows

1. *"Recall a time when you rejected someone's communication."*

2. *"Recall a time when someone rejected your communication."*

3. *"Recall a time when someone rejected another's communication."*

Communication Factor: Clear-Flow

1. *"Recall a time when you communicated well with someone."*

2. *"Recall a time when someone communicated well with you."*

3. *"Recall a time when someone communicated well with others."*

Likingness Factor: Enforced Out-Flows

1. *"Recall a time when you insisted that someone like something (or someone)."*

2. *"Recall a time when someone insisted that you like something (or someone)."*

3. *"Recall a time when someone insisted others like something (or someone)."*

Likingness Factor: Enforced In-Flows

1. *"Recall a time when you insisted that someone like you."*
2. *"Recall a time when someone insisted that you like them."*
3. *"Recall a time when someone insisted that others like them."*

Likingness Factor: Inhibited Out-Flows

1. *"Recall a time when you insisted that someone dislike something (or someone)."*
2. *"Recall a time when someone insisted that you dislike something (or someone)."*
3. *"Recall a time when someone insisted that others dislike something (or someone)."*

Likingness Factor: Inhibited In-Flows

1. *"Recall a time when you rejected someone's affection (or attention)."*
2. *"Recall a time when someone rejected your affection (or attention)."*
3. *"Recall a time when someone rejected another's affection (or attention)."*

Likingness Factor: Clear-Flow

1. *"Recall a time when you liked someone."*
2. *"Recall a time when someone liked you."*
3. *"Recall a time when someone liked another."*

Agreement Factor: Enforced Out-Flows

1. *"Recall a time when you insisted that someone agree with something (or someone)."*

2. *"Recall a time when someone insisted that you agree with something (or someone)."*
3. *"Recall a time when someone insisted others agree with something (or someone)."*

Agreement Factor: Enforced In-Flows

1. *"Recall a time when you insisted that someone agree with you."*
2. *"Recall a time when someone insisted that you agree with them."*
3. *"Recall a time when someone insisted that others agree with them."*

Agreement Factor: Inhibited Out-Flows

1. *"Recall a time when you insisted that someone disagree with something (or someone)."*
2. *"Recall a time when someone insisted that you disagree with something (or someone)."*
3. *"Recall a time when someone insisted others disagree with something (or someone)."*

Agreement Factor: Inhibited In-Flows

1. *"Recall a time when you rejected someone's reality (or refused to agree with them)."*
2. *"Recall a time when someone rejected your reality (or refused to agree with you)."*
3. *"Recall a time when someone rejected another's reality (or refused to agree with them)."*

Agreement Factor: Clear-Flow

1. *"Recall a time when you agreed with someone."*
2. *"Recall a time when someone agreed with you."*
3. *"Recall a time when someone agreed with another."*

HANDLING THE "FLOW-FACTORS"

Very early on the *"Backtrack,"* we approached existence from a much more *"All-Pervading"* and *"All-Knowing"* state—but, of course, that did not offer us much room to experience any kind of *game-conditions*. Therefore, to have some genuine sense of *interest* or *curiosity* in our lives, it was necessary for us to first *agree* to *"Not-Know"* at least *something* about something.

Where it comes to our encounters in this present *Shared-Game Universe*, the *"Not-Knowing"* is what allows the original *barriers* to exist. The *agreed-upon* boundaries defined (for example) by an individual's own *"Mind"* or a *"Wall"* restrict the *apparent* "ALL-ness" that could be potentially experienced or *Known*. These *barriers* only exist, of course, within the *"reality"* of the *Game* or *Universe*; they are not *"actual"* conditions.

Most of the time, the "upsets" and "imbalances" that affect us in our daily lives come from the *perception* that there are too many *factor-breaks* and *barriers*. An individual can also become "inhibited," "antagonistic" or "bored" by not having enough *randomness* too. Therefore, a happy healthy life is comprised of just enough *"game"* for one's own *tolerance*. Of course, increasing that *tolerance* is quite desirable for *Ascension*.

We often approach the *Game of Life*, then, from some degree of *"Not-Knowing."* Our *attention* is then directed by *interest* or *curiosity*. This generates an *energy-flow*, such as we have described in our lessons concerning the *factors*, *flow-types* and *circuits*. When there is "good" communicat-

ion and *agreement* (*&tc.*), life plays out with minimal disruption and difficulty.

But, *this Universe* is quite obviously not built upon *Self-Honesty*—and *fragmentation* runs rampant in the typical "*Human*" experience. Often times, an individual does not fully "*connect*" and instead encounters some degree of *resistance*. Assuming one continues to be *interested* in spite of this, an increase or amplification (intensity) of the *energy-flow* (or *attention-flow*) is necessary to overcome the *resistance*. This is where the individual tends to find some trouble.

As we have spoken of previously in this lesson, when an individual starts to apply *energy* against *energy*, and *force* against *force*, they begin to engage with further *barriers* and more solid *game-conditions*. In the example just given: if an *interest* or *curiosity* (in someone or something) is *inhibited*, it promotes an *increased desire* and a more impactful (or solid) energetic or material *effort* to overcome the *resistance*. This brings us far and below the operating levels of high-power *Alpha-Thought* and true *Self-determinism*.

Continuing our example: if the individual is unsuccessful in accomplishing what they *desire*, and is unable (or unwilling) to abandon the pursuit, the directed energy (of the flow) must increase further in its material solidity, and *effort* will now be applied to *enforce* or *insist upon* the intended *flow*. This is when an individual falls low enough in *Awareness* to start operating *automatically* on *reactive-mechanisms* (*fragmentation*).

Once an individual starts *reactively* operating on *fragmentation*, their *efforts* generally are unsuccessful—quite frankly because they are intensely applying *effort* in the first place. Assuming this fails to deliver the *desired results* (or *effect*), as it usually does, the individual switches to the *inhibition* side of the *flow*. The "thing" or "person" (*terminal*) is now so "*highly charged*" that the *intentional effort* becomes "to get away" from it (or to "keep it away"). But, the individual is still *intensely* and *compulsively* "connected" to it.

Rather than confronting a thing "*As-It-Is*," the typical *reactive-response* to "getting away from" something that is *highly charged* (or undesirable) is to "make nothing" of *it* —to treat it as if it were "not a thing." It is no longer experienced "*As-It-Is*," and yet there is still a "*flow*" that an individual now starts rejecting furiously. This is the point when one angrily "doesn't want" anything to do with the thing they formerly *desired*. And in low-level cases, the individual will go as far as to act out against (or even destroy) it.

This systematic sequence we have described may apply to any of the three *flow-factors*. This is the theory demonstrated in the *processes* found in the previous section— which provides a systematic means of sorting out the originating source of *turbulence* and *fragmentation* for such *flows* encountered in everyday life.

When the *Alpha-Spirit* decides to "*Not-Know*" something in order to have a "game"—an application of *attention* and *interest* (or *curiosity*) is what essentially provides something to "do" ("be" or "have") in existence. It provides enough *randomness* for one to enjoy their life. However, when this is not handled properly—or when the "player" is not operating clearly in *Self-Honesty*—succumbing to a level of *intense desire* only imposes further *fragmentation* and *barriers*. Life suddenly becomes more difficult to manage.

The "upsets" of life are treated as *breaks* (or *barriers*) in the *flow-factors*. For *Solo-Processing*, a *Seeker* first looks over the *incident* or *occurrence* carefully, *spotting* and *confronting* whatever is accessible. To make the *fragmentation* available for *processing*, the first step is simply seeing "*What-Is*," and not focusing on any *confusions* or other unresolved parts of the experience.

These *flow-factor* "upsets" are only *systematically processed* when a *Seeker* is distanced from the source of the *break*—when the *turbulence* is not actively *restimulated* by the environment. If a *Seeker* is still too *emotionally charged-up* (hysterically upset, *&tc.*) from a recent *occurrence*, then the first step must include alternating "*spotting something in the incident*" and "*spotting something in the (room)*" until further *processing* can begin.

When the *Seeker* is ready for *defragmentation* of the *upset*, the instructions are: consider each of the *flow-factors* —"*communication*," "*likingness*" and "*agreement*"—and determine which was the most significantly present in the *upset*. Once you have spotted the *factor*, consider what *flow-type* is attached to it; primarily, is it being "*enforced*" or "*inhibited*"?

Familiarity with PCL from the previous section should help you to identify the "quality" of the particular *flow* you are handling for this form of *processing*. Note that in this lesson, we have also added "*Not-Knowing*," "*interest/curiosity*" and "*desire*" to this "scale" of potential *flow-types*. These other three types are sequentially "above" (or precede) "*enforcement*," "*inhibition*" and "*refusal*" on the "scale."

When the correct combination of *factor* and *flow-type* is *spotted* for an *upset*, there should be some sense of *relief* or *emotional release.* If not, it is possible that either the *factor* or *flow-type* (or both) was assessed wrongly. In that case, you simply return to the beginning of these steps and try again. If you "stir" up too much *turbulence* in trying to find out, simply add the alternating PCL of "*spotting something in the room,*" so that not all of your attention is fixed on the *restimulation* of the *upset.*

The *relief/release* gained by this *spotting* technique (above) may be partial or complete. If it's complete, then you can move off onto another *process*, or *end-session*. If, however, it is only partially *defragmented* (but there is some *relief* from *spotting* the correct *factor* and *flow-type*), then you continue with additional steps (below).

First, *spot* the "*flow-direction*" or "*circuit.*" For example: did *you inhibit* someone's *communication*, or did someone else *inhibit* yours? Then, *spot* exactly what "*communication*" was *inhibited* (for example); and then *spot* what you "did" (*action*) and what you "decided" (*thought*) in the incident. If possible, also *spot* any lingering upper-level *considerations* and *postulates* you made as a result of the experience.

If this technique doesn't provide a complete *defragmentation*, it is likely that there is an *earlier incident* of a similar nature that is connected to it "on a chain." All you need to do is *spot* the *earlier incident* and *run* through the steps again.

If at any time during this *processing*, things şeem to "feel better" and then suddenly the *fragmentation* seems "more solid" again, you likely *ran* the *process* too long. Simply alternate: *spotting* the moment you had experienced the *end-point*, and *spotting* something in the room, until you get to "feeling better" again.

MORE ON "BARRIERS"

Let us now take a moment and examine a holistic view, reviewing what we have *realized*, from all the lessons composing our *Professional Course* for the "*Pathway to Ascension*" so far.

In the beginning, an *Alpha-Spirit* goes "*out-of-communication*" *knowingly* and *selectively*. While this, at first, is a matter of personal preference or choice, it is generally encouraged or influenced from an "outside" or "other-determined" source. This is undesirable, because once an individual goes "*out-of-communication*" too far, they then are suddenly easier to *control* from outside "environmental" and "other-determined" sources.

Once a being is "*out-of-communication*" there is a greater chance for encountering things that they don't *like*; and the individual begins *protesting* them, instead of *confronting* them. This is when *fragmentation* sets in; the individual starts to *compulsively create* (and "*postulate*") things into existence from a state of *protest* (as in "*communicating*" a *protest*)—and this leads to the experience of *problems.*

In typical cases of *fragmentation* (*e.g. the Human Condition*), an individual experiencing "*problems*" will apply increasingly low-level *efforts* to "solve" the *problem*. This leads to committing "*Harmful-Acts*," which now have to be *held-out* (and other actions that are now consciously *held-back*), leading to only further and further *withdrawal* from existence "*As-It-Is*" and the development of additional *barriers*, such as we have described throughout this lesson.

More *recently* on the *Backtrack*, an *Alpha-Spirit* identifies *Self* more closely as a "material body" that can be hurt (because *Self* "*considers*" that *Self* can be hurt as a result). Prior to this, earlier in the *game*, the *Alpha-Spirits* were more like "*demi-gods*" that could really only annoy or tease one another—or mess up each others *creations*. But while *knowingly* operating as an "*eternal being*," they knew that nothing permanent could affect each other. Of course, we have fallen quite far in our *Awareness* of this native state, and have found ourselves essentially "stuck" within these *creations*.

From the perspective of the *Human Condition*, it often *appears* as though we have "good reason" for the various *upsets* we encounter in life—especially since our recent history on the *Backtrack* has included great "pain" and "destruction." It *appears* as though the *breaks* and *barriers* (of *factors* and *flows*) are a direct result from the various harms that have been present in this lifetime and in recorded history.

The truth is that these *breaks* and *barriers* are connected to "chains" of *fragmentation* that occurred much earlier in our *Spiritual Timeline* (or *Backtrack*); back when we were still "above" the level of *considering* ourselves able to be actually harmed (in a mortal sense). We could, however, still feel "hurt" from, for example, "*refusal to communicate*" or "*rejected affections*," *&tc*. That is how a lot of the "mess" in existence came into being: first the *breaks* and *barriers*, and then the "*wars*."

At first, a *Seeker* may question the *systematic accuracy* of the "*fragmentation pattern*" we have just described. After all, personal tastes ("*likes*") often differ, and there are many people presently not "*communicating*" with each other—and this does not seem to present a *problem* or *upset* in itself. But, that is not what we mean in this lesson. Simply not having a lot of *flow*-activity is not the same as having a *factor-break*, in that it does not carry the *"emotional charge"* or a *"chain of fragmentation"* with it.

The *factor-breaks* we experience in this lifetime as *upsets* only occur because there is already existing *"charge"* or *"fragmentation"* present on the line. A proper or "clear" use of the *factors* is usually sufficient to "dissipate" or "eliminate" most of what accumulates in everyday life. For example: when we "listen to," "care for," "help," or otherwise engage well with others and our environment, our lives bring "happiness."

On the other hand, when the *factor-flows* are "cut" or "broken" abruptly—either by *enforcement* or *inhibition*—any of the "charge" that would be "relieved" by a proper *flow*, suddenly "backs up" (or becomes a "blockage") as an *energetic-mass*. This is what prompts a personal response, originating from the *reactive-mechanisms* of *fragmentation*, that seem so excessively out of proportion to what a present situation calls for.

As we close this lesson, it is important to understand: it is not the *factor-flows* themselves that cause *fragmented charge* on one's track, but an individual's own *compulsions* and *inhibitions* in regards to the *breaks* and *barriers* encountered. And this includes the *fragmentation* encountered concerning what an individual "must" or "must not" *Be, do* or *have*. And this returns us full circle to what we have covered in the earlier lessons regarding *"reach"* and *"withdrawal."*

Finally, it is only when we are in a state of Self-Honesty, with a *willingness* to *Be, do,* or *have* "anything" (without any *compulsion* or *reactive avoidance*), that we are truly *free* of the *Human Condition*—having risen far beyond the *barriers* of *upsets* and *problems* inherent in that *fragmented* state.

It is only when we can regain the high-power *Alpha-Thought* of our former native state that we will have a truly *Self-determined* and totally *free choice*. In a *fragmented state*, all *considerations* are of a "lower order" because the external "other-determined" factors of life are given more validation as a *source* of our experience of existence than we give ourselves. This is one of the things that improves for a *Seeker* as they progress in their *processing levels* of *Systemology* and prepare *Self* to again experience an *Ascended* state.

ADVANCED PROCESSING

The following *systematic processes* are traditionally applied after using the PCL given in *Lesson-6*: "*Spot three places you are not.*" The purpose is to more easily assume a *viewpoint* that is "*exterior*" to the *body* (or even the confines of the *Physical Universe*) and be able to "*spot*" things from that *viewpoint*.

For these *processes*, simply *imagine* that you are hovering above, and freely able to move about, a city or populated area. At this *processing level*, we are not concerned with how accurate or vivid these "*remote*" *perceptions* (or "*ZU-Vision*") may be. Just "*spot*" things anyway; *imagining* them (or how they *might* be) as needed.

Attacking

1. *"Spot three people that you are not attacking."*

2. *"Spot three people that are not attacking you."*

3. *"Spot three people that are not attacking others."*

Hatred

1. *"Spot three people that you do not hate."*

2. *"Spot three people that do not hate you."*

3. *"Spot three people that don't hate each other."*

Ordering

1. *"Spot three people that you are not giving orders to."*

2. *"Spot three people that are not giving you orders."*

3. *"Spot three people that aren't giving orders to others."*

Beauty

1. *"Spot three things you find beautiful to look at."*

2. *"Spot three things someone else would find beautiful to look at."*

3. *"Spot three people looking at beautiful things."*

Safety

1. *"Spot three places where your body would be safe."*

2. *"Spot three places where someone else would be safe."*

3. *"Spot three places where other bodies would be safe."*

0. *"Spot three places where you would be safe."*

LESSON EIGHT: CONQUEST OF ILLUSION

PERSONAL INTEGRITY

Our practice of *Systemology* toward *Ascension* is effective for the simple fact that: at the core, in our most basic state, the *Alpha-Spirit* is actually quite "righteous" and "good." This is what allows us to rehabilitate *abilities* and restore the level of *Awareness*. Nothing is being "added" to *Self* on the *Pathway*; it is the "additives" that are being "removed," and in doing so, removing the *barriers* and *blockages* of our true state.

We have already treated the preliminaries of "*Eliminating Barriers*" in our previous lesson (booklet). In this one, we continue further in this area to complete the necessary *systematic processing* for *Systemology Level-3*. Much of the material found in this lesson (booklet) is based on a book found in our *Systemology Core*, titled: "*The Way of the Wizard*."

At the inception of *Shared-Game Universes*, *Alpha-Spirits* went to great lengths to "trick" and "deceive" one another. This is because, during our early experiences as *god-like* beings—before we considered our *Self* to be attached to any kind of "*body*" that could be harmed—"deception" and "trickery" is about all that you could really do against another *god-like* being.

"*Illusions*" were originally created for fun and entertainment—similar to going to the "movies" or attending a "stage magic" show. Remember that, at basic, we as *Alpha-Spirits*, have a uniquely strong fondness for "*games*." But later on, more recently on the *Backtrack* of our *Spiritual Existence*, things became more serious as these "illusions" started to be used as a means of *entrapping* and *enslaving* each other.

This is not an easy area for many to handle or *process*. As such, many *Seekers* that have started upon the *Pathway* often fall by the wayside, never progressing beyond this *processing level*. It is a lot to *confront* for some *Seekers*, which is why we only earn success with these areas after first completing the work provided in the previous lessons (booklets) of this *Professional Course*.

"CONFUSION" AND "FALSEHOOD"

It is sometimes quite challenging to differentiate between *truth* and *falsehood*, or to effectively *dispel illusion*. We have all had a lot of experience in mastering these skills. *Trickery* and *illusion* is also used to *conceal* the true native state that is available to us as *Alpha-Spirits*.

The *fragmentation* that stands as a *barrier* to the highest *realizations* of ourselves is almost entirely composed of *illusion* and *falsehood*. Our experience on the *Backtrack*, in this lifetime and others, has afforded us a great bit of *fragmentation* concerning all sides of this area—what has been done to us and what we have done to others—and also what we have observed with others handling others.

Some of what would appear to be "*basic processing*" in this lesson is really intended to simply get a *Seeker* to actually recognize the facets associated with these various areas that have contributed to holding them back from the full *realization* of *Self*, in *Self-Honesty*, free of *fragmentation*, *compulsion* and *inhibition*.

When an individual *"Knows,"* they are not susceptible to *"falsehood."* Only after an *Alpha-Spirit* agrees to *"Not-Know"* (in order to have a *game*) will they fall prey to *trickery* and *deception*. One of the ways in which an *Alpha-Spirit* might be fooled, is through *misdirection* of *attention* —which is to say *"distraction."* It is this mechanism that allows a "stage magician" to fool an audience—and concealing what is *really* going on.

There is also the matter of *"confusion."* When one is in a state of *"confusion,"* they are quite likely to reinforce the solidity of *fragmentation* in their lives by reaching for the wrong piece of "data" in which to stabilize or orient themselves.

States of *"confusion"* are so undesirable that an individual will grab a hold of anything that might bring resolution to the situation without fully analyzing and reviewing the content. And this is one way in which a person might be misled or manipulated to agree with *"false data."*

One of the most basic ways an individual overcomes *illusion* and *falsehood* is by *recognizing* it *"As-It-Is."* This becomes increasingly simpler to do as a *Seeker* elevates their level of *Actualized Awareness*.

At high levels of personal application, *Awareness* is sufficient enough to unravel and disperse *fragmentation* "on sight"—but only if *actually* "seen" *As-It-Is*, and not some false alteration of whatever *"It"* is.

The following *basic processes* employ the *"Analytical Recall"* technique described in former lessons. Their function is to help *realize* the type of areas we want to *resurface*, or bring into view, for *Systemology Level-3*.

Falsehood — Trickery/Fighting

1. *"Recall a time when you tricked someone into fighting."*
2. *"Recall a time when someone tricked you into fighting."*
3. *"Recall a time when someone tricked others into fighting."*

Falsehood — Distraction/Attention

1. *"Recall a time when you intentionally shifted someone's attention."*
2. *"Recall a time when someone intentionally shifted your attention."*
3. *"Recall a time when someone intentionally shifted another's attention."*

Falsehood — Confusion

1. *"Recall a time when you confused someone."*
2. *"Recall a time when someone confused you."*
3. *"Recall a time when someone confused others."*

As an additional exercise in identifying the *ideas* that we have used to resolve or reduce *confusion*, consider the following *process*:

A1. *"Recall a confusion."*
A2. *"What 'idea' resolved or reduced that confusion?"*

DEFRAGMENTING "FALSEHOOD"

There are always people in our societies that "instigate" or propagate *confusion*, *falsehood* and *suppression*. This is not unique to only life here on this planet. There are innumerable times in history when *conflict* or *confusion* was encouraged for someone's personal gain or to eliminate an opponent. In many ways this is an inherent part of *games* that involve *"players"* who perceive themselves as in "competition" with each other.

Information is easily mishandled—or *miscommunicated.* Whether intentionally given or otherwise, such *misinformation* or *false-data* is inherently *fragmentation.* It contributes to our having a false *perception* of our environment, and subsequently our making inaccurate evaluations when participating—*acting* and *doing* things —in existence. This *fragmentation* reduces our *Awareness* and the clarity of our memory.

One of the ways in which *falsehood* is spread, is by *"Passing the Buck."* We mean when *"blame"* is misplaced onto some individual, family, group, or society—race, country, *&tc*. This is a *misdirection* of *attention* (*Awareness*) from a "true source" to a "false source" (thereby disguising the *real* origination of an action).

Another commonly used tactic is to *misdirect* or *"shift"* the data about the date/timing of an event—replacing actual data with invented data. This not only obscures the facts, but can also either *"diminish"* or *"exaggerate"* the *significance* of the data—such as representing *events* as being "longer ago" than they actually are, *&tc*.

Sometimes efforts to *"shift significance"* of facts are more direct. For example, someone might overtly (visibly or obviously) "downplay" or "exaggerate" the perceived importance (*significance*) of some data for their own covert (hidden) purposes or gains. This also occurs when someone acts to *embarrass, belittle* or *shame* an individual. Such *"suppressive"* individuals tend to hinder expressions of *creativity* and *ability*.

The following *processes* employ *"Analytical Recall"* to assist a *Seeker* in *recognizing* and *identifying* the presence of *"misdirection"* and *"manipulation"* in their own lives (and in memory, or on the *Backtrack*).

Processes like these *may* lead to some new *end-realization*; but more often, directly *confronting* the *imprinted* memory of such areas of *fragmentation* will result in *relief/release* and increased *Awareness.*

Falsehood—Shifting Blame

1. *"Recall a time when you tried to shift blame onto another."*
2. *"Recall a time when someone tried to shift blame onto you."*
3. *"Recall a time when someone tried to shift blame onto another."*

Falsehood—Shifting Time

1. *"Recall misleading someone about the time when something occurred."*
2. *"Recall someone misleading you about the time when something occurred."*
3. *"Recall someone misleading others about the time when something occurred."*

Falsehood—Shifting Significance

1A. *"Recall a time when you exaggerated the importance of something."*
1B. *"Recall a time when you downplayed the importance of something."*
2A. *"Recall a time when someone else exaggerated the importance of something."*
2B. *"Recall a time when someone else downplayed the importance of something."*

Falsehood — Embarrassment/Shame

1. *"Recall a time when you made another embarrassed."*
2. *"Recall a time when someone made you embarrassed."*
3. *"Recall a time when someone made another embarrassed."*

Falsehood — Accusations

1. *"Recall a time when you falsely accused someone."*
2. *"Recall a time when someone falsely accused you."*
3. *"Recall a time when someone falsely accused another (or others)."*

Falsehood — Encouraged Conflict

A. *"Spot a time when you were told that someone (or something) was bad."*
B. *"Identify the person that told you that."*
C. *"Did that person have personal interests invested? How so?"*

Falsehood — True/False

A. *"Spot something you were told that you found out to be true."*
B. *"Spot something you were told that you found out to be false."*

Falsehood — Manipulation

1. *"How have you misled (or manipulated) another?"*
2. *"How has another misled (or manipulated) you?"*
3. *"How has another misled (or manipulated) others?"*

HANDLING "SUPPRESSION"

As a *Seeker* progresses along the *Pathway*, more and more of the "hiccups" and "upsets" of the *Human Condition* — and experience of life in general — are able to be *confronted "As-It-Is"* (how things actually are).

Most of us have encountered at least one individual in our present lifetime that continually "acts" toward *creating* challenges and difficulties for you personally. Some individuals apply this *effort* to larger groups of people, or even society as a whole. Those maintaining "higher" levels of *Actualized Awareness* are generally in a better position to handle such people directly, or at least the situations that they are *creating*.

A highly *Self-Actualized* individual doesn't succumb to suppression. It is possible, sometimes, to "win an enemy over" (getting them to accept/agree with your "side" or *reality*). If you can maintain your own "integrity" or "position" strongly or long enough, sometimes it is sufficient to "drive them off," or simply "wait them out" until the matter is dropped. But, this all requires being free of *automatic reactive-responses*.

There are also those unexpected or intense situations when an individual quickly becomes *overwhelmed* — the sense that one has become *too much* the *effect* of the environment (or external source). The best course of action in this case is to remove yourself from the overwhelming influence and "catch your breath" in a safe position. This isn't a *withdrawal*, when ultimately, the situation will still have to be *confronted "As-It-Is."*

One reason why these persons and situations are so challenging for many individuals to handle, is because, quite often: the "present occurrence" *restimulates* much older (and longer) *"chains of fragmentation"*—stirring up *turbulence* from similar situations in the past that were left unresolved (*not-confronted*). This is what influences our succumbing to external "pressures."

Enslavement and *Domination* are *games* as old as the *Backtrack* itself. In fact, there are some individuals that carry *"fragmented purposes"* with them that are left over from *old games* (often from "past lives") they still have a lot of their *Awareness* "stuck" on. They are still "playing" or "acting" in *this life* and *this game*, the "*roles*" or "*goals*" that they clung to long ago. That creates difficulties for others also playing on *this field*.

While it is easy to identify the more obvious situations we have encountered, it is the "*covert attacks*" and "*passive-aggressive*" *efforts* to *dominate* or *invalidate* us, that many *Seekers* are unprepared to handle in life. The most dangerous of our supposed "opponents" are those that specifically attempt to "*suppress*" our progress, gains, creative ability, and of course, advancement on the *Pathway-to-Ascension*.

A *personality* or *player* that is a *suppressive-type* will consistently try to *invalidate*—or "make less of"—you. Their general aim for *control* is to "*stop action.*" Encounters with such types tend to leave us feeling "depressed" or "hopeless"—and yet they may also attempt to make us, in some way, "dependent" on them.

It is senseless to try to avoid all encounters with *domination* and *competition* in this *Universe*. It is an inherent part of the *"roles"* and *"goals"* perceived as part of the *game*; but many players are perceiving and operating with *"fragmented purposes"*—and they do not improve our experience of the *Game of Life* in any way.

The most desirable position (or solution) is to simply be in such "good condition" (as an *Actualized Seeker*) that these "external" (*other-determined*) *efforts* do not have enough "impact" to *invalidate* you—that your level of *Awareness* "exceeds" the degree or level of *energy* or *force* being "thrown at" you, and it may be essentially dissolved *"As-It-Is."* There is no reason to react or engage with further *energy* or *force*, which are of a "lower" order or condition of *existence* and *creation* than a *Self-Actualized Alpha-Spirit* is capable of.

DEFRAGMENTING "SUPPRESSION"

As mentioned above, most *suppressive control* is aimed at *"stopping motion"* (or action). While there are ways of being *constructively critical*, most *criticism* is intended to reduce or "make nothing" of another's *efforts* or *creations*. The following *basic processes* will help in identifying these *occurrences*. [We will employ the word *"spot"* in these PCL to more accurately apply this *processing* to the full *Backtrack*.]

Suppression—Stops

1. *"Spot a time when you stopped someone."*

2. *"Spot a time when someone stopped you."*

3. *"Spot a time when someone stopped another (or others)."*

0. *"Spot a time when you stopped yourself."*

Suppression—Criticism

1. *"Spot a time when you criticized someone."*

2. *"Spot a time when someone criticized you."*

3. *"Spot a time when someone criticized another (or others)."*

0. *"Spot a time when you criticized yourself."*

Suppression—Invalidation

1. *"Spot a time when you 'made nothing' of someone."*

2. *"Spot a time when someone 'made nothing' of you."*

3. *"Spot a time when someone 'made nothing' of another (or others)."*

0. *"Spot a time when you 'made nothing' of yourself."*

It is not uncommon to find that encounters with a very *"suppressive-type"* during childhood can remain influential later on in life—even when that individual is no longer present. But that is how *imprints* work. When *Solo-Processing* the following exercise, use your *notebook* or *Flight-log* to record the data from each PCL-question. List multiple answers (if necessary) to make sure you have answered each fully.

A. *"Is there anyone around whom you seem to become 'sick' shortly after seeing them?"*

B. *"Is there anyone who is continuously critical of you?"*

C. *"Is there anyone who is often telling you how 'bad' other people are?"*

D. *"Is there anyone who continuously 'stops' you?"*

E. *"Is there anyone who continuously 'invalidates' you?"*

F. *"Is there anyone who often provides 'false' information?"*

G. *"Is there anyone who often 'makes nothing' of your efforts?"*

If you find yourself writing the same name on several lists, then *run* the following *processes* using that name as the *"terminal"* (blank space) in the PCL. If there are multiple names that frequently appear, then *run* those names as *terminals* too (each as their own series of *processes*). There is no "judgment" applied here about someone else's *intentions* toward us. The very fact that their name shows up frequently on these "lists" is sufficient to indicate there is enough *charge* present (as *fragmentation*) to be *run* as *processing*.

The following series of *processes* begins with a familiar one (from previous lessons) regarding *"help."* The purpose is not to enforce actually helping someone, but to restore the free choice (that is not overridden by *fragmentation*). *Considerations* of *"help"* also assist in breaking down the *barriers* of negative reactive emotion so that a *Seeker* is better able to actually confront the source of *suppression "As-It-Is."*

Suppressive Terminal—Help

1. *"How could you help ---?"*
2. *"How could --- help you?"*
3A. *"How could --- help others?"*
3B. *"How could others help ---?"*

Suppressive Terminal—Problems

1A. *"What 'problem' have you been to ---?"*
1B. *"What have they done about that?"*
2A. *"What 'problem' has --- been to you?"*
2B. *"What have you done about that?"*
3A. *"What 'problem' has --- been to others?"*
3B. *"What have others done about that?"*

4A. *"What 'problem' have others been to ---?"*

4B. *"What have they done about that?"*

Suppressive Terminal—Hold-Outs

1. *"What haven't you said to ---?"*

2. *"What hasn't --- said to you?"*

3. *"What hasn't --- said to others?"*

Suppressive Terminal—Actions

1. *"What have you done to ---?"*

2. *"What has --- done to you?"*

3A. *"What has --- done to others?"*

3B. *"What have others done to ---?"*

Suppressive Terminal—Invalidation

1. *"How have you 'invalidated' ---?"*

2. *"How has --- 'invalidated' you?"*

3A. *"How has --- 'invalidated' others?"*

3B. *"How have others 'invalidated' ---?"*

Each of the next three *processes* contains six alternating PCL. They are *run* using *"Analytical Recall"* techniques—although in this case, there may sometimes not be any available answer for a certain question. Any *turbulence* or *resistance* attached may then be handled using what you learned about *factors* in *Lesson-7*.

Trouble Sources—Likingness Factor

1A. *"Is there a time when you rejected their affection (or attention)?"*

1B. *"Is there a time when they rejected your affection (or attention)?"*

2A. *"Is there a time when you insisted that they like you?"*

2B. *"Is there a time when they insisted that you like them?"*

3A. *"Is there a time when you did like them?"*

3B. *"Is there a time when they did like you?"*

Trouble Sources—Communication Factor

1A. *"Is there a time when you rejected their communication?"*

1B. *"Is there a time when they rejected your communication?"*

2A. *"Is there a time when you insisted that they listen to you?"*

2B. *"Is there a time when they insisted that you listen to them?"*

3A. *"Is there a time when you communicated well with them?"*

3B. *"Is there a time when they communicated well with you?"*

Trouble Sources—Agreement Factor

1A. *"Is there a time when you refused to agree with them?"*

1B. *"Is there a time when they refused to agree with you?"*

2A. *"Is there a time when you insisted that they agree with you?"*

2B. *"Is there a time when they insisted that you agree with them?"*

3A. *"Is there a time when you did agree with them?"*

3B. *"Is there a time when they did agree with you?"*

Trouble Sources—Handling

A. *"What could you confront about ---?"*

B. *"What action of --- could you be responsible for?"*

C. *"What about --- could you be at cause over?"*

"JUSTIFICATION" & "RESPONSIBILITY"

Although we have discussed *"justification"* and *"responsibility"* briefly in passing up to this point of the *Pathway*, it is here at the end of *Systemology Level-3* that they are handled more directly. Although these words may appear commonly used, for *systematic processing*, we are primarily concerned with automatic reactivity regarding *compulsive action* (or *compulsive reach*) and *avoidance of action* (or *reactive withdrawal*).

The concepts of *"reach"* and *"withdrawal"* are familiar to us (by this point of the *Professional Course*), but to this, we also add the *"willingness to be responsible."* And by this, we don't mean "being blamed for things." We are speaking of a much higher-level of *"responsibility"*—as in: *"willingness* to be *at cause* over things."

Whenever an individual does something that they consider wrong—whether intentionally or otherwise—there is an *automatic* tendency to attempt to *"justify"* these actions. We do this when *communicating* about such things to others (assuming we don't *hold-out* on the information altogether)—but we also communicate these *"justifications"* to ourselves, and those *considerations* continue to affect us in the future.

In systematic terms: *justification* is a mishandling of *imprinting* or *"charge"* accumulated from an event (and possibly connected like a "chain" to similar events occurring earlier on the *Backtrack*). It strengthens the influence of *fragmentation*, because the "experiential data" is being *altered* rather than *confronted "As-It-Is"*—meaning: *reality* is being presented or perceived as *other than* it *actually is;* the worldview is distorted.

Maintaining (or *compulsively creating*) *"justifications"* or *"falsehoods"* conflicts with the state of *Self-Honesty* sought as a means of *Ascension*. Maintaining any kind of *"false data"* or *fragmented thought* also leads an individual toward *fragmented actions* that are then used to support (or prove) the *justifications*.

The following *processes* are best *run* as "listing exercises," so be sure to have your *notebook* or *Flight-log* handy. They assist in later bringing a *primary "justification consideration"* into view (which the *Seeker* is operating with the most during this lifetime)—which is the *end-point* of *Systemology Level-3*.

Justification—General

1A. *"What have you done to another?"*

1B. *"How did you justify that?"*

2A. *"What has another done to you?"*

2B. *"How have they justified that?"*

3A. *"What has someone done to others?"*

3B. *"How have they justified that?"*

Justification—Excuses

A1. *"What do you often use as an excuse?"*

A2. *"What do others often use as an excuse?"*

B1. *"How could you survive without excuses?"*

B2. *"How could others survive without excuses?"*

Willingness—Improvement

1. *"What are you willing to improve?"*

2. *"What are you willing to allow others to improve?"*

3A. *"What would someone be willing to have you improve?"*

3B. *"What would someone be willing to allow others to improve?"*

Willingness—Responsibility

A1. *"What could you be responsible for?"*

A2. *"What could another be responsible for?"*

B1. *"What would be acceptable to be irresponsible about?"*

B2. *"What would be acceptable for another to be irresponsible about?"*

[*and then run*]

1. *"Spot a time when you made someone be responsible."*

2. *"Spot a time when someone made you be responsible."*

3. *"Spot a time when someone made another (or others) be responsible."*

[*and finally, run alternately (until the "glee" of "irresponsibility" is discharged)*]

A. *"Get a sense of the joy of responsibility."*

B. *"Get a sense of the joy of irresponsibility."*

DEFRAGMENTING "JUSTIFICATION"

For most of our participation in *Shared-Game Universes*, *Alpha-Spirits* have been operating from a point of *fragmentation*. There is a mistaken, albeit *implanted*, "idea" or "goal" that we must be in *competition* with one another—that *"there can be only one"* or *"only one will survive."* There is, of course, no *actual* truth to this.

In order to reclaim the memory and abilities of our "past," it is necessary to be able to *confront* our actions (and the actions of others) in the "past" without *regret*, without *withdrawing* from the *imprints*, and without resorting to *justification* and *falsehood* (*altering* them) in order to make them more manageable. In *systematic processing*, we take some of the pressure off a *Seeker* by alternating PCL with *spotting* more positive things.

Domination—General

A. *"How have you dominated others?"*

B. *"Spot a way to enhance others."*

Domination—Stopping

A. *"How have you stopped others?"*

B. *"Spot a way to help others excel."*

Domination—Inhibition

A. *"How have you inhibited the survival of others?"*

B. *"Spot a way to aid the survival of others."*

"Domination" and *"Superiority"* are not the only *games* available to *Alpha-Spirits*. There are *better games* at higher levels of existence. However, in *this* present version of a *Physical Universe ("Beta-Existence")*—where physical *energy* and *force* are quite solid and supreme—these *games* are inherently the most common.

The type of "artificial" *fragmentation* that is *"implanted"* as *reality-agreements* for this *Universe*, instills a certain pattern of *"roles"* and *"goals"* for *this* particular *game*. This means that *all* of us have *something* that we use in order to gain our *"superiority"* over others—and we refer to this as a *"justification consideration."*

This primary *"justification consideration"* will be some basic characteristic that we emphasize in exclusion to other things—so it *should* be easy to *recognize*. The *consideration* that we are after is also quite basic in structure. It will be a *basic goal*, such as: "to be holy" or "being intelligent" or "to be strong," *&tc*. Whatever it is, it is treated in *processing* as an "item" used to make yourself "*superior*" to others.

It takes this far along the *Pathway*—the amount of *Actualized Awareness* gained by this point of *systematic processing*—in order to *confront* such a *consideration* "*As-It-Is.*" The average *Human* will quickly *withdraw* from handling such things. But even the most "*Enlightened*" among us will still have this "*item*" on their "*track*"—the key difference being that they may have risen above the tendency to use it *against* others.

Although a more complete understanding of *games*, *goals* and the *Universes* representing them, is generally earned in the most *upper-levels* of *Systemology*, it may be easily stated here that: employing your best characteristics in the low-grade *games* of *force* and *superiority* is quite "*unenlightened.*" It causes a gradual deterioration of *abilities* and abandonment of a *goal* because of the *Harmful-Acts* that are required to maintain that specific type (or "*personality-role*") of "*superiority*" and "*rightness*" for "*dominance.*"

Identifying and *recognizing* this primary "*justification consideration*" is not only necessary for completing *Systemology Level-3*, but is also the critical "*Key*" that "unlocks" (what we refer to as) the "*Backtrack*" for *upper-level processing* and additional "passes" through the *Professional Course* material.

The *game* of "*goals*" and "*roles*" extends back many "lifetimes" and many *Universes*. There is even an observable "systematic pattern" behind the way one *personality-type* and/or *goal* is abandoned, requiring the individual to shift over to another that has not already deteriorated. So this particular "item" we are looking for is likely to be the same for a certain amount of former "lifetime" experiences, but not necessarily many (relatively speaking, compared to the larger scope of things).

For achieving a basic state of "*Beta-Defragmentation*," we primarily emphasize *this* lifetime. But, there are higher applications of this same *Professional Course* after it is completed once—such as additional "*Alpha-Defragmentation*" of the *Backtrack*. For present purposes, however, it is important to prefix certain PCL (such as our "search and discovery" of the primary "*justification consideration*") with "*In this lifetime...*" Later on, a *Seeker* can explore the *Backtrack* further.

It is important to approach this final area of *Systemology Level-3* with care, because accuracy is the only way to effectively gain any stable progress from it. A *Seeker* should be in a state of high *Awareness* (having achieved "good" results from all former *processing*), be well rested (and alert), free of any actively *restimulative* sources of *fragmentation*, and finally, *interested* and *willing* to actually "discover" the "answer."

For this exercise, *list* your "answers" clearly. It's important not to do this while tired, because if you suddenly feel "heavy" or "tired" while *listing*, then you know you have *listed* too many answers—and that the basic answer you're looking for is already on the *list*. If after *listing* for a while, you start to feel "irritated" or "restimulated," then you still haven't put the answer you're looking for on the *list* yet.

Although this is a *listing exercise*, your *list* is not intended to be very long—in fact, you may *realize* what the answer is quite quickly. But, the basic instruction is to *list* "answers" in your *notebook* (or *flight-log*) below where you have written out the "question" (PCL). You continue to *list* until you feel you have "*The Answer*" or you feel comfortable that you have *listed* enough.

When you find "*The Answer*," this exercise is complete. If you're unsure which it is among your *list*, then go through it and consider each one in turn. When one doesn't seem like it's the right answer, put an "X" next to it, so you don't have to keep considering it. If at any point while checking your *list*, you suddenly *recognize* "*The Answer*," then you stop working with the *list*. And, of course, if the *list* seems incomplete, you can always add to your *listed* answers until you've completed the exercise.

The "*Question*" (PCL) is:

"*In this lifetime, what makes you superior to others?*"

Then, when you have "*The Answer*," write it in capital letters in your *notebook* (or *log*) and underline it. Take that "item" and use it to complete the next *process*. *Run* the following three PCL in alternation.

A. "*How does --- make you superior?*"
B. "*How could you use it to make yourself right?*"
C. "*How could you use it to make others wrong?*"

On the other side: we also want to find out what it is about others that you are (or might be) using against them. This might or might not relate to the "*roles*" and "*goals*" attached to the previously discovered "*justificat-*

ion consideration." To find out, a *Seeker* performs another *listing exercise* (using the same basic instructions as before). This time, the PCL-*question* is:

"In this lifetime, what is it about others that makes them so wrong?"

If you aren't satisfied with the resulting answers, there is another way of using *processing*-PCL for a "search and discovery" (related to the previous exercise) which is:

"In this lifetime, what do you use to make others wrong?"

All of the exercises/*processes* in this section focus on finding out a *Seeker's "justification consideration"* (which is also tied to the *"roles"* and *"goals"* they are playing at in this lifetime). What it generally comes down to is a *basic consideration* that "others are evil," "others are stupid," or "they're weak," *&tc*. [These examples would respectively apply to *goals/roles* of "being good," "being intelligent," and "being strong."]

To *defragment* the *"justification consideration,"* we want to systematically untangle the *"negative"* associations of using our abilities against others, while still retaining the original skill ("intelligence" or "strength," *&tc*).

The following *processes* are not *run* as simple alternating PCL. A *Seeker runs* a single PCL for as long as it continues to produce answers, then shifts to the second to get as many answers for that one, and then shifts back to the first PCL, and so on until the influential "intensity" of the *consideration* is dispersed (falls away).

Justification Consideration — Right/Wrong
  A. *"Spot ways that --- would make you right."*
  B. *"Spot ways that --- would make others wrong."*

Justification Consideration—Domination

A. *"Spot ways that --- would help you escape domination."*

B. *"Spot ways that --- would help you dominate others."*

Justification Consideration—Survival

A. *"Spot ways that --- would aid your survival."*

B. *"Spot ways that --- would hinder the survival of others."*

The influential "intensity" that we speak of is the sense that the *consideration* is "true." When it is first treated in *processing*, the *consideration* may actually seem very much like the "truth" about "why people are the way they are"—and a *justification* for "why we are the way we are." By *spotting* this *consideration* with high-level *Awareness*, the "*charge*" behind the idea or concept (as being "true") starts to dissipate or disperse. A *Seeker* then *realizes* that this is a falsely held "belief" that keeps them from *Self-Honesty*.

Assisting or "helping" others improve in the same area as your "*justification consideration*" is one way that this *defragmentation* is maintained even after *processing sessions*. It also helps to keep the "*goals*" and "*skills*" themselves from "deteriorating." For example: if your *goal* is "to be strong" (or a *role* of "being strong") and you viewed others as "wrong" for being "weak," the solution is to help others become "stronger," *&tc.*

This area is a very critical area for rehabilitation of other spiritual abilities and for rising above the limitations inherent in the standard-issue *Human Condition*. Therefore, a *Seeker* should not pass by this "checkpoint" on the *Pathway* without making certain that the "*justification consideration*" is properly found and *defragmented*. Such completes a *Seeker's processing* for *Systemology Level-3*.

SYSTEMOLOGY GLOSSARY

A-for-A (one-to-one) : an expression meaning that what we say, write, represent, think or symbolize is a direct and perfect reflection or duplication of the actual aspect or thing—that "A" is for, means and is equivalent to "A" and not "a" or "q" or "!"; in the relay of communication, the message or particle is sent and perfectly duplicated in form and meaning when received.

actualization : to make actual, not just potential; to bring into full solid Reality; to realize fully in *Awareness* as a "thing."

affinity : the apparent and energetic *relationship* between substances or bodies; the degree of *attraction* or repulsion between things based on natural forces; the *similitude* of frequencies or waveforms; the degree of *interconnection* between systems.

agreement (reality) : unanimity of opinion of what is "thought" to be known; an accepted arrangement of how things are; things we consider as "real" or as an "is" of "reality"; a consensus of what is real as made by standard-issue (common) participants; what an individual contributes to or accepts as "real"; in *Systemology*, a synonym for "*reality.*"

alpha : the first, primary, basic, superior or beginning of some form; in *Systemology*, referring to the state of existence operating on spiritual archetypes and postulates, will and intention "exterior" to the low-level condensation and solidity of energy and matter as the 'physical universe'.

alpha-spirit : a "spiritual" *Life*-form; the "true" *Self* or I-AM; the *individual*; the spiritual (*alpha*) *Self* that is animating the (*beta*) physical body or "*genetic vehicle*" using a continuous *Lifeline* of spiritual ("*ZU*") energy; an individual spiritual (*alpha*) entity possessing no physical mass or measurable waveform (motion) in the Physical Universe as itself, so it animates the (*beta*) physical body or "*genetic vehicle*" as a catalyst to experience *Self*-determined causality in effect within the *Physical Universe*; a singular unit or point of *Spiritual Awareness* that is *Aware* that it is *Aware*.

alpha thought : the highest spiritual *Self-determination* over creation and existence exercised by an Alpha-Spirit; the Alpha range of pure *Creative Ability* based on direct postulates and considerations of *Beingness*; spiritual qualities comparable to "thought" but originating in Alpha-existence (at "6.0") independently superior to a *beta-anchored* Mind-System, although an Alpha-Spirit may use Will ("5.0") to carry the intentions of a postulate or consideration ("6.0") to the Master Control Center ("4.0").

apparent : visibly exposed to sight; evident rather than actual, as presumed by Observation; readily perceived, especially by the senses.

archetype : a "first form" or ideal conceptual model of some aspect; the ultimate prototype of a form on which all other conceptions are based.

ascension : actualized *Awareness* elevated to the point of true "spiritual existence" exterior to *beta existence*. An "Ascended Master" is one who has returned to an incarnation on Earth as an inherently *Enlightened One*, demonstrable in their actions—they have the ability to *Self-direct* the "Spirit" as *Self* and maintain consciousness beyond this existence as a personal identity continuum with the same *Self-directed* control and communication of Will-Intention that is exercised, actualized and developed deliberately during one's present incarnation.

assessment : an analysis or synthesis of collected information, usually about a person or group, in relation to an *assessment scale*.

associative knowledge : significance or meaning of a facet or aspect assigned to (or considered to have) a direct relationship with another facet; to connect or relate ideas or facets of existence with one another; a reactive-response image, emotion or conception that is suggested by (or directly accompanies) something other than itself; in traditional systems logic, an equivalency of significance or meaning between facets or sets that are grouped together, such as in $(a + b) + c = a + (b + c)$; in Systemology, erroneous associative knowledge is assignment of the same value to all facets or parts considered as related (even when they are not actually so), such as in $a = a, b = a, c = a$ and so forth without distinction.

attention : active use of *Awareness* toward a specific aspect or thing; the act of "attending" with the presence of *Self*; a direction of focus or concentration of *Awareness* along a particular channel or conduit or toward a particular terminal node or communication termination point; the Self-directed concentration of personal energy as a combination of observation, thought-waves and consideration; focused application of *Self-Directed Awareness*.

awareness : the highest sense of-and-as Self in knowing and being as I-AM (the *Alpha-Spirit*); the extent of beingness directed as a POV experienced by Self as knowingness.

axiom : a fundamental truism of a knowledge system, esp. *logic*; all *maxims* are also *axioms*; knowledge statements that require no proof because their truth is self-evident; an established law or systematic principle used as a *premise* on which to base greater conclusions of truth.

beta (awareness) : all consciousness activity ("*Awareness*") in the "Physical Universe" (KI) or else *beta-existence*; *Awareness* within the range of the *genetic-body*, including material thoughts, emotional responses and physical motors; personal *Awareness* of physical energy and physical matter moving through physical space and experienced as "time"; the *Awareness* held by *Self* that is restricted to a physical organic *Lifeform* or "*genetic vehicle*" in which it experiences causality in the *Physical Universe*.

beta (existence) : all manifestation in the "Physical Universe" (KI); the "Physical" state of existence consisting of vibrations of physical energy and physical matter moving through physical space and experienced as "time"; the conditions of *Awareness* for the *Alpha-spirit* (*Self*) as a physical organic *Lifeform* or "*genetic vehicle*" in which it experiences causality in the *Physical Universe*.

beta-defragmentation : toward a state of *Self-Honesty* in regards to handling experience of the "Physical Universe" (*beta-existence*); an applied spiritual philosophy (or technology) of Self-Actualization originally described in the text "*Crystal Clear*" (*Liber-2B*), building upon theories from "*Systemology: The Original Thesis.*"

catalyst : something that causes action between two systems or aspects, but which itself is unaffected as a variable of this energy communication; a medium or intermediary channel.

chakra : an archaic Sanskrit term for "wheel" or "spinning circle" used in *Eastern* wisdom traditions, spiritual systems and mysticism; a concept retained in Systemology to indicate etheric concentrations of energy into wheel-mechanisms that process *ZU* energy at specific frequencies along the *ZU-line*, of which the *Human Condition* is reportedly attached *seven* at various degrees as connected to the Gate symbolism.

channel : a specific stream, course, current, direction or route; to form or cut a groove or ridge or otherwise guide along a specific course; a direct path; an artificial aqueduct created to connect two water bodies or water or make travel possible.

charge : to fill or furnish with a quality; to supply with energy; to lay a command upon; in *Systemology*—to imbue with intention; to overspread with emotion; application of *Self-directed (WILL)* "intention" toward an emotional manifestation in beta-existence; personal energy stores and significances entwined as fragmentation in mental images, reactive-response encoding and intellectual (and/or) programmed beliefs; in traditional mysticism, to intentionally fix an energetic resonance to meet some degree, or to bring a specific concentration of energy that is transferred to a focal point, such as an object or space.

circuit : a circular path or loop; a closed-path within a system that allows a flow; a pattern or action or wave movement that follows a specific route or potential path only; in *Systemology*, "*communication processing*" pertaining to a specific flow of energy or information along a channel; *see* also "*feedback loop.*"

communication : successful transmission of information, data, energy (&tc.) along a message line, with a reception of feedback; an energetic flow of intention to cause an effect (or duplication) at a distance; the personal energy moved or acted upon by will or else 'selective directed attention'; the 'messenger action' used to transmit and receive energy across a medium; also relay of energy, a message or signal—or even locating a personal POV (viewpoint) for the Self—along the *ZU-line*.

compulsion : a failure to be responsible for the dynamics of control—starting, stopping or altering—on a particular channel of communication and/or regarding a particular terminal in existence; an energetic flow with the appearance of being 'stuck' on the action it is already doing or by the control of some automatic mechanism.

concept : a high-frequency thought-wave representing an "idea" which persists because it is not restricted to a unique space-time; an abstract or tangible "idea" formed in the "Mind" or *imagined* as a means of understanding, usually including associated "Mental Images"; a seemingly timeless collective thought-theme (or subject) that entangles together facets of many events or incidents, not just a single significant one.

condense (condensation) : the transition of vapor to liquid; denoting a change in state to a more substantial or solid condition; leading to a more compact or solid form.

condition : an apparent or existing state; circumstances, situations and variable dynamics affecting the order and function of a system; a series of interconnected requirements, barriers and allowances that must be met; in "contemporary language," bringing a thing toward a specific, desired or intentional new state (such as in "conditioning"), though to minimize confusion about the word "condition" in our literature, *Systemology* treats "contemporary conditioning" concepts as imprinting, encoding and programming.

conflict : the opposition of two forces of similar magnitude along the same channel or competing for the same terminal; the inability to duplicate another POV; a thought, intention or communication that is met with an opposing counter-thought or counter-intention that generates an energetic cluster.

confront : to come around in front of; to be in the presence of; to stand in front of, or in the face of; to meet "face-to-face" or "face-up-to"; additionally, in *Systemology*, to fully tolerate or acceptably withstand an encounter with a particular manifestation or encounter.

consciousness : the energetic flow of *Awareness*; the Principle System of *Awareness* that is spiritual in nature, which demonstrates potential interaction with all degrees of the Physical Universe; the *Beingness* component of our existence in *Spirit*; the Principle System of *Awareness* as *Spirit* that directs action in the Mind-System.

consideration : careful analytical reflection of all aspects; deliberation; determining the significance of a "thing" in relation to similarity or dissimilarity to other "things"; evaluation of facts and importance of certain facts; thorough examination of all aspects related to, or important for, making a decision; the analysis of consequences and estimation of significance when making decisions; in *Systemology*, the postulate or Alpha-Thought that defines the state of beingness for what something "*is.*"

continuity : being a continuous whole; a complete whole or "total round of"; the balance of the equation ["–120" + "120" = "0" *&tc.*]; an apparent unbroken interconnected coherent whole; also, as applied to Universes in *Systemology*, the lowest base consideration of space-time or commonly shared level of energy-matter apparent in an existence, or else the lowest degree of solidity or condensation whereby all mass that exists is identifiable or communicable with all other mass that exists; represented as "0" on the *Standard Model* for the Physical Universe (*beta-existence*), a level of existence that is below Human emotion, comparable to the solidity of "rocks" and "walls" and "inert bodies."

continuum : a continuous enduring uninterrupted sequence or condition; observing all gradients on a *spectrum*; measuring quantitative variation with gradual transition on a spectrum without demonstrating discontinuity or separate parts.

control (general) : the ability to start, change or start some action or flow of energy; the capacity to originate, change or stop some mode of human behavior by some implication, physical or psychological means to ensure compliance (voluntarily or involuntarily).

control (systems) : communication relayed from an operative center or organizational cluster, which incites new activity elsewhere in a system (or along the *ZU-line*)

defragmentation : the *reparation* of wholeness; collecting all dispersed parts to reform an original whole; a process of removing "*fragmentation*" in data or knowledge to provide a clear understanding; applying techniques and processes that promote a *holistic* interconnected *alpha* state, favoring observational *Awareness* of continuity in all spiritual and physical systems; in *Systemology*, a "*Seeker*" achieving an actualized state of basic "*Self-Honest Awareness*" is said to be *beta-defragmented*, where as *Alpha-defragmentation* is the rehabilitation of the *creative ability*, managing the *Spiritual Timeline* and the POV of *Self* as Alpha-Spirit (I-AM); see also "*Beta-defragmentation*."

degree : a physical or conceptual *unit* (or point) defining the variation present relative to a *scale* above and below it; any stage or extent to which something *is* in relation to other possible positions within a *set* of "*parameters*"; a point within a specific range or spectrum; in *Systemology*, a *Seeker's* potential energy variations or fluctuations in thought, emotional reaction and physical perception are all treated as "*degrees*."

dramatization / dramatize : a vivid display or performance as if rehearsed for a "play" (on stage); a *'circuit'* recording *'imprinted'* in the past and, once restimulated by a facet of the environment, the individual "replays" it as through reacting to it in the present (and identifying that reality as present reality); acts, actions and observable behaviors that demonstrate identification with a particular character type, "phase" or personality program; a motivated sequence-chain, implant series or imprinted cycle of actions—usually irrational or counter-survival—repeated by an individual as it had previously happened to them; a reoccurring or reactively triggered out-flow, communication or action that indicates an individual "occupying" a particular *'Point-of-View'* (*POV*)—typically fixed to a specific (past) identification (identity) that is space-time locatable (meaning a point where significant *Attenergy* —enough to compulsively create and maintain a POV—is "stuck" or "hung up" on the *BackTrack*).

dynamic (systems) : a principle or fixed system which demonstrates its *'variations'* in activity (or output) only in constant relation to variables or fluctuation of interrelated systems; a standard principle, function, process or system that exhibits *'variations'* and change simultaneously with all connected systems; each *'Sphere of Existence'* is a dynamic system, systematically affecting (supporting) and affected (supported) by other *'Spheres'* (which are also dynamic systems).

emotional encoding : the readable substance/material (data) of *'imprints'*; associations of sensory experience with an *imprint*; perceptions of our environment that receive an *emotional charge*, which form or reinforce facets of an *imprint*; perceptions recorded and stored as an *imprint* within the "emotional range" of energetic manifestation; the formation of an energetic store or charge on a channel that fixes emotional responses as a mechanistic automation, which is carried on in an individual's *Spiritual Timeline* (or personal continuum of existence).

encompassing : to form a circle around, surround or envelop around.

end point : the moment when the goal of a process has been achieved and to continue on with it will be detrimental to the gains; the finality of a process when the *Seeker* has achieved their optimum state from the current cycle (whether or not they run through it again at a later date with a different level of *Awareness* or knowledge base doesn't change the fact that it has flattened the standing wave

enforcement : the act of compelling or putting (effort) into force; to compel or impose obedience by force; to impress strongly with applications of stress to demand agreement or validation; the lowest-level of direct control by physical effort or threat of punishment; a low-level method of control in the absence of true communication.

evaluate : to determine, assign or fix a set value, amount or meaning.

existence : the *state* or fact of *apparent manifestation*; the resulting combination of the Principles of Manifestation: consciousness, motion and substance; continued *survival*; that which independently exists; the *'Prime Directive'* and sole purpose of all manifestation or Reality; the highest common intended motivation driving any "*Thing*" or *Life*.

exterior : outside of; on the outside; in *Systemology*, we mean specifically the POV of *Self* that is *'outside of'* the *Human Condition*, free of the physical and mental trappings of the Physical Universe; a metahuman range of consideration; see also '*Zu-Vision*'.

external : a force coming from outside; information received from outside sources; in *Systemology*, the objective *'Physical Universe'* existence, or *beta-existence*, that the Physical Body or *genetic vehicle* is essentially *anchored* to for its considerations of locational space-time as a dimension or POV.

facets : an aspect, an apparent phase; one of many faces of something; a cut surface on a gem or crystal; in *Systemology*—a single perception or aspect of a memory or "*Imprint*"; any one of many ways in which a memory is recorded; perceptions associated with a painful emotional (sensation) experience and "*imprinted*" onto a metaphoric lens through which to view future similar experiences; other secondary terminals that are associated with a particular terminal, painful event or experience of loss, and which may exhibit the same encoded significance as the activating event.

faculties : abilities of the mind (individual) inherent or developed.

feedback loop : a complete and continuous circuit flow of energy or information directed as an output from a source to a target which is altered and return back to the source as an input; in *General Systemology*—the continuous process where outputs of a system are routed back as inputs to complete a circuit or loop, which may be closed or connected to other systems/circuits; in *Systemology*—the continuous process where directed *Life* energy and *Awareness* is sent back to *Self* as experience, understanding and memory to complete an energetic circuit as a loop.

flow : movement across (or through) a channel (or conduit); a direction of active energetic motion typically distinguished as either an *in-flow*, *out-flow* or *cross-flow*.

fragmentation : breaking into parts and scattering the pieces; the *fractioning* of wholeness or the *fracture* of a holistic interconnected *alpha* state, favoring observational *Awareness* of perceived connectivity between parts; *discontinuity*; separation of a totality into parts; in *Systemology*, a person outside a state of *Self-Honesty* is said to be *fragmented*.

game : a strategic situation where a "player's" power of choice is employed or affected; a parameter or condition defined by purposes, freedoms and barriers (rules).

general systemology ("systematology") : a methodology of analysis and evaluation regarding the systems—their design and function; organizing systems of interrelated information-processing in order to perform a given function or pattern of functions.

genetic-vehicle : a physical *Life*-form; the physical (*beta*) body that is animated/controlled by the (*Alpha*) *Spirit* using a continuous *Lifeline* (ZU); a physical (*beta*) organic receptacle and catalyst for the (*Alpha*) *Self* to operate "causes" and experience "effects" within the *Physical Universe*.

gradient : a degree of partitioned ascent or descent along some scale, elevation or incline; "higher" and "lower" values in relation to one another.

hold-back : withheld communications (esp. actions) such as "*Hold-Outs*"; intentional (or automatic) withdrawal (as opposed to reach); Self-restraint (which may eventually be enforced or automated); not reaching, acting or expressing, when one should be; an ability that is now restrained (on automatic) due to inability to withhold it on Self-determinism alone.

hold-outs : in photography, the numerous snapshots/pictures withheld from the final display or professional presentation of the event; withheld communications; in Utilitarian Systemology—energetic withdrawal and communication breaks with a "*terminal*" and its *Sphere of Existence* as a result of a "*Harmful-Act*"; unspoken or undiscovered (hidden, covert) actions that an individual withholds communications of, fearing punishment or endangerment of *Self-preservation* (*First Sphere*); the act of hiding (or keeping hidden) the truth of a "*Harmful-Act*"; a refusal to communicate with a *Pilot*; also "*Hold-Back*."

holistic : the examination of interconnected systems as encompassing something greater than the *sum* of their "parts."

Human Condition : a standard default state of Human experience that is generally accepted to be the extent of its potential identity (*beingness*)—currently treated as *Homo Sapiens Sapiens,* but which is scheduled for replacement by *Homo Novus*.

identification : the association of *identity* to a thing; a label or fixed data-set associated to what a thing is; association "equals" a thing, the "equals" being key; an equality of all things in a group, for example, an "apple" identified with all other "apples"; the reduction of "I-AM"-*Self* from a *Spiritual Beingness* to an "identity" of some form.

identity : the collection of energy and matter—including memory—across a "*Spiritual Timeline*" that we consider as "I" of *Self*, but the "I" is an individual and not an identification with anything other than *Self* as *Alpha-Spirit*.

imagination : the ability to create *mental imagery* in one's Personal Universe at will and change or alter it as desired; the ability to create, change and dissolve mental images on command or as an act of will; to create a mental image or have associated imagery displayed (or "conjured") in the mind that may or may not be treated as real (or memory recall) and may or may not accurately duplicate objective reality; to employ *Creative Abilities* of the Spirit that are independent of reality agreements with beta-existence.

imprint : to strongly impress, stamp, mark (or outline) onto a softer 'impressible' substance; to mark with pressure onto a surface; in *Systemology*, the term is used to indicate permanent Reality impressions marked by frequencies, energies or interactions experienced during periods of emotional distress, pain, unconsciousness, loss, enforcement, or something antagonistic to physical (personal) survival, all of which are are stored with other reactive response-mechanisms at lower-levels of *Awareness* as opposed to the active memory database and proactive processing center of the Mind; an experiential "memory-set" that may later resurface—be triggered or stimulated artificially—as Reality, of which similar responses will be engaged automatically; holographic-like imagery "stamped" onto consciousness as composed of energetic *facets* tied to the "snap-shot" of an experience.

imprinting incident : the first or original event instance communicated and *emotionally encoded* onto an individual's "*Spiritual Timeline*" (recorded memory from all lifetimes), which formed a permanent impression that is later used to mechanistically treat future contact on that channel; the first or original occurrence of some particular *facet* or mental image related to a certain type of *encoded response*, such as pain and discomfort, losses and victimization, and even the acts that we have taken against others along the Spiritual Timeline of our existence that caused them to also be *Imprinted*.

inhibited : withheld, held-back, discouraged or repressed from some state.

"in phase" : see "*phase alignment.*"

intention : the directed application of Will; to intend (have "in Mind") or signify (give "significance" to) for or toward a particular purpose; in *Systemology* (from the *Standard Model*)—the spiritual activity at WILL (5.0) directed by an *Alpha Spirit* (7.0); the application of WILL as "Cause" from a higher order of Alpha Thought and consideration (6.0), which then may continue to relay communications as an "effect" in the universe.

interior : inside of; on the inside; in *Systemology*, we mean specifically the POV of *Self* that is fixed to the *'internal' Human Condition,* including the *Reactive Control Center* (RCC) and Mind-System or *Master Control Center* (MCC); within *beta-existence*.

internal : a force coming from inside; information received from inside sources; in *Systemology*, the objective *'Physical Universe'* experience of *beta-existence* that is associated with the Physical Body or *genetic vehicle* and its POV regarding sensation and perception; from inside the body; within the body.

invalidate : decrease the level or degree or *agreement* as Reality.

knowledge : clear personal processing of informed understanding; information (data) that is actualized as effectively workable understanding; a demonstrable understanding on which we may 'set' our *Awareness*—or literally a "know-ledge."

Master-Control-Center (MCC) : a perfect computing device to the extent of the information received from "lower levels" of sensory experience/perception; the proactive communication system of the "*Mind*"; a relay point of active *Awareness* along the Identity's *ZU-line*, which is responsible for maintaining basic *Self-Honest Clarity* of *Knowingness* as a *seat of consciousness* between the *Alpha-Spirit* and the secondary "*Reactive Control Center*" of a *Lifeform* in *beta existence*; the Mind-center for an *Alpha-Spirit* to actualize cause in the *beta existence*; the analytical *Self-Determined* Mind-center of an *Alpha-Spirit used* to project *Will* toward the genetic body; the point of contact between *Spiritual Systems* and the *beta existence*; presumably the "*Third Eye*" of a being connected directly to the *I-AM-Self*, which is responsible for *determining* Reality at any time; in *Systemology*, this is plotted at (4.0) on the continuity model of the *ZU-line*.

mental image : a subjectively experienced "picture" created and imagined into being by the Alpha-Spirit (or at lower levels, one of its automated mechanisms) that includes all perceptible *facets* of totally immersive scene, which may be forms originated by an individual, or a "facsimile-copy" ("snap-shot") of something seen or encountered; a duplication of wave-forms in one's Personal Universe as a "picture" that mirror an "external" Universe experience, such as an *Imprint*.

methodology : a complete system of applications, methods, principles and rules to compose a *'systematic'* paradigm as a "whole"—esp. a field of philosophy or science.

misappropriated : put into use incorrectly; to apply ineffectively or as unintended by design or definition.

objective : concerning the "external world" and attempts to observe Reality independent of personal "subjective" factors.

one-to-one : see "*A-for-A.*"

optimum : the most favorable or ideal conditions for the best result; the greatest degree of result under specific conditions.

organic : as related to a physically living organism or carbon-based life form; energy-matter condensed into form as a focus or POV of Spiritual Life Energy (*ZU*) as it pertains to beta-existence of *this* Physical Universe (*KI*).

paradigm : an all-encompassing *standard* by which to view the world and *communicate* Reality; a standard model of reality-systems used by the Mind to filter, organize and interpret experience of Reality.

parameters : a defined range of possible variables within a model, spectrum or continuum; the extent of communicable reach capable within a system or across a distance; the defined or imposed limitations placed on a system or the functions within a system; the extent to which a Life or "thing" can *be*, *do* or *know* along any channel within the confines of a specific system or spectrum of existence.

patterns (probability patterns) : observation of cycles and tendencies to predict a causal relationship or determine the actual condition or flow of dynamic energy using a holistic systemology to understand Life, Reality and Existence as opposed to isolating or excluding perceived parts as being mutually separate from other perceived parts.

perception : internalized processing of data received by the *senses*; to become *Aware of* via the senses.

personality (program) : the total composite picture an individual "identifies" themselves with; the accumulated sum of material and mental mass by which an individual experiences as their timeline; a "beta-personality" is mainly attached to the identity of a particular physical body and the total sum of its own genetic memory in combination with the data stores and pictures maintained by the Alpha Spirit; a "true personality" is the Alpha Spirit as Self completely defragmented of all erroneous limitations and barriers to consideration, belief, manifestation and intention.

phase (identification) : in *Systemology,* a pattern of personality or identity that is assumed as the POV from *Self*; personal identification with artificial "personality packages"; an individual assuming or taking characteristics of another individual (often unknowingly as a response-mechanisms); also "*phase alignment.*"

phase alignment or "***in phase***" : to be in synch or mutually synchronized, in step or aligned properly with something else in order to increase the total strength value; in *Systemology*, alignment or adjustment of *Awareness* with a particular identity, space or time; perfect *defragmentation* would mean being "in phase" as *Self* fully conscious and Aware as an Alpha-Spirit *in* present *space* and *time*, free of synthetic personalities.

physics : regarding data obtained by a material science of observable motions, forces and bodies, including their apparent interaction, in the Physical Universe (specific to this *beta-existence*).

physiology : a material science of observable biological functions and mechanics of living organisms, including codification and study of identifiable parts and apparent systematic processes (specific to agreed upon makeup of the *genetic vehicle* for this *beta-existence*).

pilot : a professional steersman responsible for healthy functional operation of a ship toward a specific destination; in *Systemology*, an intensive trained individual qualified to specially apply *Systemology Processing* to assist other *Seekers* on the *Pathway.*

point-of-view (POV) : a point to view from; an opinion or attitude as expressed from a specific identity-phase; a specific standpoint or vantage-point; a definitive manner of consideration specific to an individual phase or identity; a place or position affording a specific view or vantage; circumstances and programming of an individual that is conducive to a particular response, consideration or belief-set (paradigm); a position (consideration) or place (location) that provides a specific view or perspective (subjective) on experience (of the objective).

postulate : to put forward as truth; to suggest or assume an existence *to be*; to state or affirm the existence of particular conditions; to provide a basis of reasoning and belief; a basic theory accepted as fact; in *Systemology*, "Alpha-Thought"—the top-most decisions or considerations made by the Alpha-Spirit regarding the "*is-ness*" (what things "are") about energy-matter and space-time.

potentiality : the total "sum" (collective amount) of "latent" (dormant—present but not apparent) capable or possible realizations; used to describe a state or condition of what has not yet manifested, but which can be influenced and predicted based on observed patterns and, if referring to beta-existence, Cosmic Law.

presence : the quality of some thing (energy/matter) being "present" in space-time; personal orientation of *Self* as an *Awareness* (*POV*) located in present space-time (environment) and communicating with extant energy-matter.

Prime Directive : a "spiritual" implant program that installs purposes and goals into the personal experience of a Universe, esp. any *Beta-Existence* (whether a 'Games Universe' or a 'Prison Universe'); intellectually treated as the "Universal Imperative" in some schools of moral philosophy; comparable to "Universal Law" or "Cosmic Ordering."

"process-out" : to reduce *emotional encoding* of an *imprint* to zero; to dissolve a *wave-form* or *thought-formed* "solid" such as a "*belief*"; to completely run a *process* to its end, thereby *flattening* any previous *waves* of *fragmentation* that are obstructing the *clear channel* of *Self-Awareness*; also referred to as "processing-out"; to discharge all previously held emotionally encoded imprinting or erroneous programming and beliefs that otherwise fix the free flow (wave) to a particular pattern, solid or concrete "*is*" form.

processing command line (PCL) or **command line** : a directed input; a specific command using highly selective language for *Systemology Processing*; a predetermined directive statement (cause) intended to focus concentrated attention (effect).

processing, systematic : the inner-workings or "through-put" result of systems; in *Systemology*, a methodology of applied spiritual technology used toward personal Self-Actualization; methods of selective directed attention, communicated language and associative imagery that targets an increase in personal control of the human condition.

reactive control center (RCC) : the secondary (reactive) communication system of the "*Mind*"; a relay point of *Awareness* along the Identity's *ZU-line*, which is responsible for engaging basic motors, biochemical processes and any *programmed automated responses* of a living *beta* organism; the reactive Mind-Center of a living organism relaying communications of *Awareness* between causal experience of *Physical Systems* and the "*Master Control Center*"; it presumably stores all emotional encoded imprints as fragmentation of "chakra" frequencies of *ZU* (within the range of the "*psychological/emotive systems*" of a being), which it may *react* to as Reality at any time; in *Systemology*, this is plotted at (2.0) on the continuity model of the *ZU-line*.

reality : see "*agreement.*"

realization : the clear perception of an understanding; a consideration or understanding on what is "actual"; to make "real" or give "reality" to so as to grant a property of "beingness" or "being as it is"; the state or instance of coming to an *Awareness*; in *Systemology*, "gnosis" or true knowledge achieved during *systematic processing*; achievement of a new (or "higher") cognition, true knowledge or perception of Self; a consideration of reality or assignment of meaning.

relative : an apparent point, state or condition treated as distinct from others.

responsibility : the *ability* to *respond*; the extent of mobilizing *power* and *understanding* an individual maintains as *Awareness* to enact *change*; the proactive ability to *Self-direct* and make decisions independent of an outside authority.

resurface : to return to (or bring up to) the "surface" of that which has previously been submerged; in *Systemology*—relating specifically to processes where a *Seeker* recalls blocked energy stored covertly as emotional "*imprints*" (by the RCC) so that it may be effectively defragmented from the "*ZU-line*" (by the MCC).

Seeker : an individual on the *Pathway to Self-Honesty*; a practitioner of *Mardukite Systemology* or *Systemology Processing* that is working toward *Spiritual Ascension*.

Self-actualization : bringing the full potential of the Human spirit into Reality; expressing full capabilities and creativeness of the *Alpha-Spirit*.

Self-determinism : the freedom to act, clear of external control or influence; the personal control of Will to direct intention.

Self-honesty : the basic or original *alpha* state of *being* and *knowing*; clear and present total *Awareness* of-and-as *Self*, in its most basic and true proactive expression of itself as *Spirit* or *I-AM*—free of artificial attachments, perceptive filters and other emotionally-reactive or mentally-conditioned programming imposed on the human condition by the systematized physical world; the ability to experience existence without judgment.

sensation : an external stimulus received by internal sense organs (receptors/sensors); sense impressions.

slate : a hard thin flat surface material used for writing on; a chalk-board, which is a large version of the original wood-framed writing slate, named for the rock-type it was made from.

spectrum : a broad range or array as a continuous series or sequence; defined parts along a singular continuum; in physics, a gradient arrangement of visible colored bands diffracted in order of their respective wavelengths, such as when passing *White Light* through a *prism*.

Spheres of Existence (dynamic systems) : a series of *eight* concentric circles, rings or spheres (each larger than the former) that is overlaid onto the Standard Model of Beta-Existence to demonstrate the dynamic systems of existence extending out from the POV of Self (often as a "body") at the *First Sphere*; these are given in the basic eightfold systems as: *Self, Home/Family, Groups,*

Humanity, Life on Earth, Physical Universe, Spiritual Universe and *Infinity-Divinity.*

spiritual timeline : a continuous stream of moment-to-moment *Mental Images* (or a record of experiences) that defines the "past" of a spiritual being (or *Alpha-Spirit*) and which includes impressions (*imprints, &tc.*) form all life-incarnations and significant spiritual events the being has encountered; in Systemology, also "*backtrack.*"

standard issue : equally dispensed to all without consideration.

Standard Model, The (systemology) : in *Systemology*—our existential and cosmological *standard model* or cabbalistic model; a "*monistic continuity model*" demonstrating *total system* interconnectivity "above" and "below" observation of any apparent *parameters*; the original presentation of the *ZU-line*, represented as a singular vertical (y-axis) waveform in space across dimensional levels or Universes (*Spheres of Existence*) without charting any specific movement across a dimensional time-graph x-axis; The Standard Model of Systemology represents the basic workable synthesis of common denominators in models explored throughout Grade-I and Grade-II material.

static : characterized by a fixed or stationary condition; having no apparent change, movement or fluctuation.

succumb : to give way, or give in to, a relatively stronger superior force.

system : from the Greek, "to set together"; to set or arrange things or data together so as to form an orderly understanding of a "whole"; also a *'method'* or *'methodology'* as an orderly standard of use or application of such data arranged together.

systematization : to arrange into systems; to systematize or make systematic.

terminal (node) : a point, end or mass on a line; a point or connection for closing an electric circuit, such as a post on a battery terminating at each end of its own systematic function; any end point or 'termination' on a line; a point of connectivity with other points; in systems, any point which may be treated as a contact point of interaction; anything that may be distinguished as an 'is' and is therefore a 'termination point' of a system or along a flow-line which may interact with other related systems it shares a line with; a point of interaction with other points.

thought-form : apparent *manifestation* or existential *realization* of *Thought-waves* as "solids" even when only apparent in Reality-agreements of the Observer; the treatment of *Thought-waves* as permanent *imprints* obscuring *Self-Honest Clarity* of *Awareness* when reinforced by emotional experience as actualized "thought-formed solids" ("*beliefs*") in the Mind; energetic patterns that "surround" the individual.

thought-habit : reoccurring modes of thought or repeated "self-talk"; essentially "self-hypnosis" resulting in a certain state.

thought-wave or **wave-form** : a proactive *Self-directed action* or reactive-response *action* of *consciousness*; the *process* of *thinking* as demonstrated in *wave-form*; the *activity* of *Awareness* within the range of *thought vibrations/frequencies* on the existential *Life-continuum* or *ZU-line*.

threshold : a doorway, gate or entrance point; the degree to which something is to produce an effect within a certain state or condition; the point in which a condition changes from one to the next.

tier : a series of rows or levels, one stacked immediately before or atop another.

time : observation of cycles in action; motion of a particle, energy or wave across space; intervals of action related to other intervals of action as observed in Awareness; a measurable wave-length or frequency in comparison to a static state; the consideration of variations in space.

timeline : plotting out history in a linear (line) model to indicate instances (experiences) or demonstrate changes in state (space) as measured over time; a singular conception of continuation of observed time as marked by event-intervals and changes in energy and matter across space.

turbulence : a quality or state of distortion or disturbance that creates irregularity of a flow or pattern; the quality or state of aberration on a line (such as ragged edges) or the emotional "turbulent feelings" attached to a particular flow or terminal node; a violent, haphazard or disharmonious commotion (such as in the ebb of gusts and lulls of wind action).

understanding : a clear 'A-for-A' duplication of a communication as 'knowledge', which may be comprehended and retained with its significance assigned in relation to other 'knowledge' treated as a 'significant understanding'; the "grade" or "level" that a knowledge base is collected and the manner in which the data is organized and evaluated.

validation : reinforcement of agreements or considerations as "real."

viewpoint : see "*point-of-view" (POV)*.

will *or* **WILL** (5.0) : in *Systemology* (from the *Standard Model*), the Alpha-ability at "5.0" of a Spiritual Being (*Alpha Spirit*) at "7.0" to apply *intention* as "Cause" from consideration or Alpha-Thought at "6.0" that is superior to "beta-thoughts" that only manifest as reactive "effects" below "4.0" and *interior* to the *Human Condition*.

willingness : the state of conscious Self-determined ability and interest (directed attention) to *Be*, *Do* or *Have*; a Self-determined consideration to reach, face up to (*confront*) or manage some "mass" or energy; the extent to which an individual considers themselves able to participate, act or communicate along some line, to put attention or intention on the line, or to produce (create) an effect.

ZU : the ancient Sumerian cuneiform sign for the archaic verb —"*to know*," "*knowingness*" or "*awareness*"; in *Mardukite Zuism and Systemology*, the active energy/matter of the "Spiritual Universe" (AN) experienced as a *Lifeforce* or *consciousness* that imbues living forms extant in the "Physical Universe" (KI); "*Spiritual Life Energy*"; energy demonstrated by the WILL of an actualized *Alpha-Spirit* in the "Spiritual Universe" (AN), which impinges its *Awareness* into the Physical Universe (KI), animating/controlling *Life* for its experience of *beta-existence* along an individual Alpha-Spirit's personal *Identity-continuum*, called a *ZU-line*.

***Zu*-Line** : a theoretical construct in *Mardukite Zuism and Systemology* demonstrating *Spiritual Life Energy* (*ZU*) as a personal individual "continuum" of Awareness interacting with all Spheres of Existence on the Standard Model of Systemology; a spectrum of potential variations and interactions of a monistic continuum or singular *Spiritual Life Energy (ZU)* demonstrated on the Standard Model; an energetic channel of potential POV and "locations" of Beingness, demonstrated in early Systemology materials as an individual Alpha-Spirit's personal *Identity-continuum*, potentially connecting *Awareness (ZU)* of *Self* with "*Infinity*" simultaneous with all points considered in existence; a symbolic demonstration of the "*Life-line*" on which *Awareness (ZU)* extends from the direction of the "Spiritual Universe" (AN) in its true original *alpha state* through an entire possible range of activity resulting in its *beta state* and control of a *genetic-entity* occupying the *Physical Universe (KI)*.

Zu-Vision : the true and basic (*Alpha*) Point-of-View (perspective, POV) maintained by *Self* as *Alpha-Spirit* outside boundaries or considerations of the *Human Condition* "Mind-Systems" and *exterior* to beta-existence reality agreements with the Physical Universe; a POV of Self *as* "a unit of Spiritual Awareness" that exists independent of a "body" and entrapment in a *Human Condition*; "spirit vision" in its truest sense.

WOULD YOU LIKE TO KNOW MORE

? ? ?

AVAILABLE FROM THE **JOSHUA FREE** PUBLISHING IMPRINT

SYSTEMOLOGY
The Pathway to Self-Honesty

The Official Introduction to
Mardukite Systemology

FUNDAMENTALS OF SYSTEMOLOGY

**The New Thought
of the 21st Century**

a basic course
by
Joshua Free

Systemology is the study of how Spiritual Beings with unlimited
power became entrapped in the Human Condition. This study is
an applied philosophy— "A Pathway to Ascension" —that charts
our way back out of the traps, freeing the true Spiritual Self to
experience higher levels of existence once again. In the simplest
terms: Systemology is the true metaphysical science of the
"Matrix." After more than a decade of development, the
"Fundamentals of Systemology" are concisely explored here in
the very first official "Basic Course" on the subject ever given by
Joshua Free for the Mardukite Academy. This collector's edition
hardcover includes all six of the original lesson-booklets for the
"Basic Course" (also available separately). It's time to discover
who you really are... because you were never "Human."

The First Official Systemology Basic Course
on Dynamic Systems of Life and Universes

AVAILABLE FROM THE **JOSHUA FREE** PUBLISHING IMPRINT

SYSTEMOLOGY
The Pathway to Self-Honesty
THE ORIGINAL UNDERGROUND INTRODUCTIONS REVISED AND REISSUED IN HARDCOVER

SYSTEMOLOGY
The Original Thesis of Mardukite New Thuoght
by Joshua Free
(*Mardukite Systemology Liber-S-1X*)

The very first underground discourses released to the "New Thought" division of the Mardukite Research Organization privately over a decade ago and providing the inspiration for rapid futurist spiritual technology called "Mardukite Systemology."

THE POWER OF ZU
Applying Mardukite Zuism & Systemology to Everyday Life
by Joshua Free
Foreword by Reed Penn
(*Mardukite Systemology Liber-S-1Z*)

A unique introductory course on Mardukite Zuism & Systemology, including transcripts from a 3-day lecture series given by Joshua Free in December 2019 to launch the Mardukite Academy of Systemology & Founding Church of Mardukite Zuism just in time for the 2020's.

AVAILABLE FROM THE **JOSHUA FREE** PUBLISHING IMPRINT

SYSTEMOLOGY
The Pathway to Self-Honesty

THE TABLETS OF DESTINY REVELATION

How Long-Lost Anunnaki Wisdom Can Change the Fate of Humanity

by Joshua Free

Mardukite Systemology
Liber-One

second edition

Discover the origins of the Pathway to Self-Honesty with the book that started it all!

In this newly revised "Revelations" Academy Edition: Rediscover the original system of perfecting the Human Condition on a Pathway that leads to Infinity. Here is a way!—a map to chart spiritual potential and redefine the future of what is means to be human.

A landmark public debut for Grade-III Systemology and the foundation stone for reaching higher and taking back control of your
DESTINY!

The revelation of 6,000 year old secrets, providing the tools and wisdom to unlock human potential...

AVAILABLE FROM THE **JOSHUA FREE** PUBLISHING IMPRINT

SYSTEMOLOGY
The Pathway to Self-Honesty

CRYSTAL CLEAR
Handbook for Seekers

*Achieving
Self-Actualization
& Spiritual Ascension
in This Lifetime*

by Joshua Free

*Mardukite Systemology
Liber-2B*

second edition

Take control of your destiny and chart the first steps
toward your own spiritual evolution.

Realize new potentials of the Human Condition with
a Self-guiding handbook for Self-Processing
toward Self-Actualization in Self-Honesty using actual
techniques and training provided for the coveted
"Mardukite Self-Defragmentation Course Program"
—once only available directly and privately from the
underground International Systemology Society.

Discover the amazing power behind the
applied spiritual technology
used for counseling and advisement in
the Mardukite Zuism tradition.

AVAILABLE FROM THE **JOSHUA FREE** PUBLISHING IMPRINT

SYSTEMOLOGY
The Pathway to Self-Honesty

METAHUMAN DESTINATIONS

The Original 2020 Professional Piloting Academy Course for Grade IV

by Joshua Free

Mardukite Systemology
Liber-Two (2C,2D,3C)
Revised 2-Volume Set

available individually

Drawing from the Arcane Tablets and nearly a year of additional research, experimentation and workshops since the introduction of applied spiritual technology and systematic processing methods, Joshua Free provides the ground-breaking manual for those seeking to correct—or "defragment"—the conditions that have trapped viewpoints of the Spirit into programming and encoding of the Human Condition.

Experience the revolutionary professional course in advanced spiritual technology for Mardukite Systemologists to "Pilot" the way to higher ideals that can free us from the Human Condition and return ultimate command and control of creation to the Spirit.

AVAILABLE FROM THE **JOSHUA FREE** PUBLISHING IMPRINT

SYSTEMOLOGY
The Gateways to Infinity

IMAGINOMICON

Accessing the Gateway to Higher Universes

A New Grimoire for the Human Spirit

by Joshua Free

Mardukite Systemology Grade-IV Metahumanism, Wizard Level-0, Liber-3D

revised edition

The Way Out. Hidden for 6,000 Years.
But now we've found the Key.
A grimore to summon and invoke, command and control,
the most powerful spirit to ever exist.
Your Self.

Access beyond physical existence.
Fly free across all Gateways.
Go back to where it all began and reclaim that
personal universe which the *Spirit* once called "*Home*."

Break free from the Matrix;
control the Mind and command the Body
from outside those systems
— because *You* were never "human" —
fully realize what it means to be a *spiritual being*,
then rise up through the Gateways to Higher Universes
and *BE*.

AVAILABLE FROM THE **JOSHUA FREE** PUBLISHING IMPRINT

SYSTEMOLOGY
The Gateway to Infinite Self-Honesty

THE WAY OF THE WIZARD

Utilitarian Systemology

A New Metahuman Ethic

by Joshua Free

Mardukite Systemology Liber-3E

Grade-IV to Grade-V transition bridge

Your ticket off of a Prison Planet...
...and a Pathway leading to Spiritual Ascension!

Accumulated involvement in dangerous situations, states of confusion, unjust destruction and being at the effect end of faulty—or—blatantly false information, all lend to fragmented purposes that may very well be painted to appear "for our own good." Instead they are non-survival or counter-survival oriented, leading us away from routes to achieve "greater heights"—higher, more ideal, states of knowingness and beingness—including the Magic Universe immediately preceding this one.

Here then is a bridge from Grade-IV to Grade-V, the next great frontier of the *Pathway* crossed by participants in the "Freedom From" workshops led by Joshua Free in 2021.

AVAILABLE FROM THE **JOSHUA FREE** PUBLISHING IMPRINT

SYSTEMOLOGY
The Gateways to Infinity

SYSTEMOLOGY-180
The Fast-Track to Ascension
A Handbook for Pilots

by Joshua Free

Mardukite Grade-V
Systemology
Liber-180

*Expert application of
all Grade-III and Grade-IV
training and techniques*

A perfected "metahuman" state for the Human Condition awaits; free of emotional turbulence, societal programming and an ability to be truly Self-Determined from the clear perspective of the actual Self, the Eternal Spirit or "I-AM" Awareness that is back of and beyond this existence—an "Angel" or "god" that has fallen only by its own considerations, by being convinced that it resides locally here on earth within a perishable human shell.

"*Systemology-180*" presents newly revised instruction from the Mardukite Academy to deliver the fastest results in climbing the Ladder of Ascension. Hundreds of exercises and techniques that progressively free you from bonds of the Human Condition and increase your spiritual horsepower enough to break the chains and attachments to the material world and an existence confined to a material body.

AVAILABLE FROM THE **JOSHUA FREE** PUBLISHING IMPRINT

SYSTEMOLOGY
The Gateways to Infinity

SYSTEMOLOGY:
BACKTRACK
Reclaiming Spiritual Power & Past-Life Memory

by Joshua Free

Mardukite Grade-V Systemology Liber-4

Transcripts of the original lectures with diagrams and glossary

We are all Spiritual Beings that have known a very long existence. Even before the evolution of Humans or Earth, we existed as other forms, in other times and spaces. We have descended down a very long *track* of potential Beingness and considerations, a *track* that parallels the allegory of "Fallen Angels" enticed by mundane bodies; only to be trapped in them and longing to *Ascend* again.

What if we could recover the long forgotten Knowingness of our past existences? What if we could reclaim our true Spiritual power that we have lost sight of? What if we could actually Backtrack our descent and return to the Source?

"Backtrack" documents the first advanced course given by Joshua Free to the Systemology Society for Grade-V. He candidly introduces the new Wizard-Level subject of Alpha-Defragmentation to Grade-III and Grade-IV alumni ready to embark on their next phase of the *Pathway*.

AVAILABLE FROM THE **JOSHUA FREE** PUBLISHING IMPRINT

IN A WORLD FULL OF "TENS" BE AN
ELEVEN

THE METAPHYSICS OF STRANGER THINGS

TELEKINESIS, TELEPATHY SYSTEMOLOGY

by Joshua Free

Mardukite Systemology Liber-011

Experimental exploratory edition

Discover the metaphysical truth about the Universe—and maybe even yourself—as we explore what lies beneath the epic saga, *Stranger Things.* You're invited to a world where fantasy, science fiction and horror unite, and games like *Dungeons and Dragons* become reality.

Uncover a world of secret "mind control" projects, just like those at *Hawkins National Laboratory*. Decades of psychedelic experiments among other developmental programs for psychic powers, remote viewing, telekinesis (psychokinesis, PK) and more are revealed. Get an inside look at the operations of a real-life underground organization pursuing the truth about rehabilitating spiritual abilities for an actual "metahuman" evolution on planet Earth.

Premiere edition available in paperback and hardcover!

AVAILABLE FROM THE **JOSHUA FREE** PUBLISHING IMPRINT

Commemorating the Mardukite 15th Anniversary!

NECRONOMICON
THE COMPLETE ANUNNAKI BIBLE
(*Deluxe Edition Hardcover Anthology*)
collected works by Joshua Free

The ultimate masterpiece of Mesopotamian magic, spirituality and history, providing a complete collection—a grand symphony—of the most ancient writings on the planet. The oldest Sumerian and Babylonian records reveal detailed accounts of cosmic history in the Universe and on Earth, the development of human civilization and descriptions of world order. All of this information has been used, since ancient times, to maintain spiritual and physical control of humanity and its systems. It has proved to be the predecessor and foundation of all global scripture-based religious and mystical traditions thereafter. These are the raw materials, unearthed from the underground, which have shaped humanity's beliefs, traditions and existence for thousands of years—right from the heart of the Ancient Near East: Sumer, Babylon and even Egypt...

AVAILABLE FROM THE **JOSHUA FREE** PUBLISHING IMPRINT

*The Original Classic Underground Bestseller Returns!
10th Anniversary Hardcover Collector's Edition.*

SUMERIAN RELIGION
Introducing the Anunnaki Gods of Mesopotamian Neopaganism

Mardukite Research Volume Liber-50

by Joshua Free

*Develop a personal relationship with Anunnaki Gods
—the divine pantheon that launched a thousand
cultures and traditions throughout the world!*

Even if you think you already know all about the Sumerian Anunnaki or Star-Gates of Babylon... * Here you will find a beautifully crafted journey that is unlike anything Humans have had the opportunity to experience for thousands of years... * Here you will find a truly remarkable tome demonstrating a fresh new approach to modern Mesopotamian Neopaganism and spirituality... * Here is a Master Key to the ancient mystic arts: true knowledge concerning the powers and entities that these arts are dedicated to... * A working relationship with these powers directly... * And the wisdom to exist "alongside" the gods, so as to ever remain in the "favor" of Cosmic Law.

"Babylonian Myth & Magic" (*Liber-51/E*) sequel also now available!

∞

PUBLISHED BY THE **JOSHUA FREE** IMPRINT REPRESENTING
**The Founding Church of Mardukite Zuism
& Mardukite Academy of Systemology**

mardukite.com

www.ingramcontent.com/pod-product-compliance
Lightning Source LLC
Chambersburg PA
CBHW072117050526
44107CB00120BA/1372/J